Those who had been scattered
preached the word wherever they went.

ACTS 8:4

Faith as a Way of Life

A VISION FOR PASTORAL LEADERSHIP

Christian Scharen

with a foreword by

Miroslav Volf

WILLIAM B. EERDMANS PUBLISHING COMPANY

GRAND RAPIDS, MICHIGAN / CAMBRIDGE, U.K.

Published 2008 by

Wm. B. Eerdmans Publishing Co.

2140 Oak Industrial Drive N.E., Grand Rapids, Michigan 49505 /

P.O. Box 163, Cambridge CB3 9PU U.K.

www.eerdmans.com

Printed in the United States of America

12 11 10 09 08   7 6 5 4 3 2 1

Library of Congress Cataloging-in-Publication Data

Scharen, Christian Batalden.

Faith as a way of life: a vision for pastoral leadership / Christian Scharen;

with a foreword by Miroslav Volf.

p.   cm.

Includes bibliographical references.

ISBN 978-0-8028-6231-0 (pbk.: alk. paper)

1. Pastoral theology.   2. Christian leadership.   I. Title.

BV4011.3.S38   2008

253 — dc22

2007048487

To

The Yale Center for Faith & Culture,

And

My colleagues in the YCFC's

Faith as a Way of Life Project, 2003-2007

Contents

CONTENTS

Foreword

From this theologian's perspective, the central challenge for pastoral ministry today concerns the most important mark of good ministry: the ability effectively to mediate faith as an integral way of life to persons, communities, and cultures. The challenge has remained basically the same throughout history, in every culture and for every community of faith. But in our time, maybe more than ever, communities of faith seem to be falling short precisely at this point. And that's where the book you are holding in your hand comes in. It seeks to mobilize pastors as well as theologians and laypeople to grapple afresh with the question of how to live out faith in our time and place.

If the number of people actively engaged in religious practices in the United States were the only relevant indicator, one could think that on the whole communities of faith were as successful today in mediating faith as a way of life as they were decades or even a century ago. And yet the faith that people embrace is, arguably, shaping their lives less and less. For the most part, the faith seems not so much an integral way of life as an energizing and consoling aura added to the business of a life shaped by factors other than faith.

An indicator of this change is a shift in language to describe religiosity. We have moved away from "faith" to "spirituality." The talk of "faith" rightly emphasizes cognitive and moral content and life in community. The talk of "spirituality," on the other hand, is cognitively and morally vague and emphasizes the empowerment and healing of autonomous individuals.

This increasing difficulty of connecting faith and life stems primarily neither from lack of effort nor from the absence of skills on the part of communities of faith and their leaders. As many sociologists of religion have noted, part of the problem is that in a market society, faith has a difficult time escaping the logic of the marketplace. It is in danger of degenerating into yet another consumer product, to be used when the need for it is felt and placed in storage or discarded when not. The problem is not so much that faith is bought and sold as a consumer product (the so-called commodification of religion), but that the smorgasbord culture in which we live exerts pressure on people to employ faith to satisfy their discrete and changing wants rather than to be the shaper of life as a whole.

The smorgasbord culture is a challenge for communities of faith. But the main problem may be that the communities of faith have not found effective ways to offer a compelling vision of an integral way of life that is worth living. Many people are seeking precisely that. They are unsatisfied with a lifestyle shaped only by two watchwords of contemporary culture: freedom and prosperity. This, too, may be signaled by the resurgent interest in spirituality as related to almost every dimension of life — from medicine to business, from arts to politics.

Why are the communities of faith ineffective in their central task? The reasons are many. One of them concerns theological education. Like all academic disciplines, theology participates in the movement of subdisciplinary differentiation and increased specialization. This is an indispensable condition of fundamental theological research. In the process, however, the overarching subject of theology and its internal unity seems to get lost. After their first experiences in churches or parachurch organizations, many young pastors are no longer certain that the long years of theological study were useful. The narrowed subjects and highly specialized theological interests of their professors do not sufficiently overlap with the everyday realities of their parishioners. Three or more years of study have handed them a tool that is sophisticated but of questionable usefulness.

To help themselves out of the predicament, many pastors revert to forms of faith they knew before their theological education began. Some turn to completely uncritical approaches to texts and concepts. These, however, soon prove intellectually implausible and woefully insufficient for the complexities of life. Others opt for an easy relevance by adopting vague religiosity and interlacing it with various secular languages, such as those of psychology or social critique. These discourses may be valuable in their own right, but in the hands of modern pastors their relation to the language of faith is often tenuous at best. In Michael Welker's apt phrases, the results of these two ways of coping with the difficulty of connecting faith with life are in the first case a self-banalization of faith, and in the second its self-secularization. Either of these approaches deprives pastors of the ability to formulate a compelling faith-based vision of life that can shape persons, communities, and cultures.

Pastors can mediate faith as a way of life only if they find it compelling themselves and if their parishioners are moved by it because it makes sense of their lives and helps them truly flourish. For help in defining a compelling faith, ministers have in the past looked to theological institutions of higher learning. It is tragic, however, that even the best of such institutions are producing very little writing about what the Christian faith has to do with the lives of lawyers or artists, manual workers or intellectuals, marketers or politicians, parents or spouses.

One of the most pressing needs of pastoral ministry, therefore, is to develop, sustain, and academically legitimize reflection on Christian faith as a way of life. In the Christian tradition such reflection is not unusual. The most effective and lasting works — of Augustine, Calvin, Luther, Wesley, Kierkegaard, Simone Weil, and others — have been effective and lasting because they offered a vision for a lived faith. Every great theology has been a vision of a way of life. Not surprisingly, the main challenge for pastoral ministry ends up being almost identical to the main challenge for theology and theological education.

Faith as a Way of Life is an account of a hands-on intellectual struggle — yes, both hands-on and intellectual! — of a group of pastors, lay people, and theologians together to explore the ways in which faith can be lived today as a way of life. Thanks to the generosity of the Lilly Endowment, I was able to convene that dynamic group. I also sketched the original vision for its work, and participated in its sessions. But it was Christian Scharen who put flesh on the bones of this project. He guided the work of the group, and did so with much wisdom born out of his own experiences as pastor and out of his training as both theologian and sociologist. His wisdom is on full display in this book as well. He has captured the spirit and the energy of the group as well as the real contributions that individual participants have made in our conversations. He also has offered a compelling analysis of the social setting that generates our difficulties with living faith as a way of life — the seeming ineluctability of modern "polytheism" and the almost irresistible attractions of contemporary individualism. Speaking in a voice of his own, Chris has given a dynamic coherence to our endeavors and done so in a way that invites others to embark upon the exciting and demanding journey of faith as a way of life.

MIROSLAV VOLF
Henry B. Wright Professor of Theology, Yale Divinity School
Founding Director of the Yale Center for Faith & Culture

Acknowledgements

It is a lovely task to give proper credit to those who played the key roles in making this project, and thus this book, come to be. First of all, I'd like to thank the key lay people, pastors, and theologians — disciples all — who worked hard on this project and gifted me with many insights I share in this book. I rejoice in their lives and ministries, and thank them for their contributions: Vince Bacote, Deb Bohlmann, Joseph Britton, Catherine Brunell, Matt Colwell, Joseph Cumming, Lillian Daniel, Gregory Ellison, Mako Fujimura, Mark Gornik, Donald Hilliard, Susan Johnson, Danielle Jones, Tony Jones, David Mahan, Skip Masback, David Miller, Mary Naegeli, Emily Pataki, Carolyn Sharp, Sally Simmel, Miroslav Volf, David Wood, Marly Youmans, and José Zeilstra. Toward the end of the writing, Mark Gornik, Greg Ellison, and Catherine Brunell read the whole, affirming my work and offering crucial feedback before the final round of revisions.

Of course, the project would not have started at all were it not for Miroslav Volf, who envisioned this project and wrote the proposal for Lilly Endowment. Likewise, the Lilly Endowment, led by Craig Dykstra's passionate and visionary commitment to Christian ministry, read and accepted the proposal. Thanks also to Dean Harry Attridge and his predecessor, Dean Rebecca Chopp, here at Yale Divinity School for consistent and strong support, and to John Wimmer, our Program Officer at Lilly, for much encouragement on his end.

ACKNOWLEDGEMENTS

I wish also to thank staff at the Yale Center for Faith and Culture throughout this project. Maurice Lee and Rachel Maxon got the project off to a good start in its initial few months. Additionally, I benefited from our administrative assistant, Lucinda Gall, and my student assistants, Sven Ensminger, Kristi Klienbeck, Allison Brancho-Tichy, and Kathryn Reklis. Kathryn, who worked with me in the first year of the project, returned at the end, reading the entire manuscript at two stages and offering remarkable stylistic and substantive suggestions throughout. This book would be much less coherent and compelling were it not for her faithful labors. Sven read the manuscript half a dozen times as he labored to put together the indexes and catch final corrections. My colleagues at the Center — Miroslav Volf, David Miller, Faith Ngunjiri, Joseph Cumming, Andy Saperstein, and Travis Tucker — all in various ways offered ongoing and sustaining friendship and the best sort of critical conversation about the shape of this work.

Jon Pott, David Bratt, and the friendly crew at Eerdmans have been helpful throughout the process, pushing me to write the best book I could for the broadest audience possible. If I have not in the end accomplished that, the fault lies with me. Bill Goettler and Maria LaSala, co-pastors at our congregation in New Haven, offered me a living example of what I have been trying to write about in this book. Bill and Maria, for your pastoral excellence, I thank God. Sonja, Isaiah, and Grace (who, even as I write this, is trying to quiz me about the "world's biggest snake"), thank you for making space for my writing in the midst of our busy lives. Sola Dei Gloria.

CHRISTIAN SCHAREN
12 *March 2007*
Commemoration of Gregory the Great, 604

CHAPTER ONE

Introduction

I'll never forget that morning. I was serving as senior pastor of an urban Lutheran church in a small New England city, and Liz, a middle-aged professional woman, wife, and mother of two, stopped me in the coffee hour following the worship service. With a wry smile she said, "Pastor Scharen, I don't know how you do it. You have to think about this religion stuff all the time! We only have to on Sundays." Her laugh betrayed that she was ribbing me, at least in part. But because we were friends, I also knew that her family commitments to leisure time meant taking the entire summer off from church, as if congregational membership was just another piece of her suburban family life interchangeable with school, soccer, or scouts. So, all jesting aside, there was something serious there.

I had two gut responses at the time, one I need to revise and one I stand by. My snap judgment was that all Liz needed was to get serious about her faith, by which I really meant attend church more regularly. Like most pastors, I was putting tremendous energy into quality Sunday worship, preaching, adult and youth education programs. I thought that if she were more serious about her faith, she'd participate in the activities that would strengthen her faith. Since she didn't, I figured, she and her family wouldn't grow deeper in their faith life. That was a mistake. I no longer as directly equate seriousness about faith with increased hours spent at church. This book gives witness to the conviction that faith is lived out in daily life. Church, therefore, plays its part — but faithfulness does not equal hours clocked under the shadow of its steeple.

However, I will stand by my second response that day: faith is not a piece of the week, containable, and useful in its place. As Liz joked about how I "think about this religious stuff all the time," I felt like I'd failed. Clearly she and her family wanted something from church. But it was largely faith as a balm, something to smooth over the difficulties of life, rather than faith as a divine transformation of our life that shapes how we engage with life's trials and joys. Balm is, of course, an important aspect of God's care for us in times of trial. Yet I wondered how I could communicate differently, so that she might see God's gift of faith as more than a balm to spread over one's life once a week. I wondered how I might make the case that God wants all of Liz's life — her "church" time as well as her time with family, at work, in the community, out shopping, or at the baseball game.

I went away that day pondering how many of us live compartmentalized lives. I mulled over the way our faith so often fails to do the work of orienting our decisions in the various parts of our lives. How often, in fact, faith simply rides to the (spiritual) rescue in times of trouble rather than serving as the beating heart pumping lifeblood through all aspects of our lives.

I hope you find yourself moaning in recognition, having had many experiences of a similar sort. But I also hope you find yourself smiling, knowing that I wrote this book having struggled to do that which I write about in its pages. I have also talked with many pastoral leaders about their struggles, and tried to learn from them as well. Despite the strong temptation to write a book that purports to give you the answers, I have not. Such books overestimate the potential of transplanting ideas from one context to another. Before you set the book down, however, I hasten to add that I do intend this book to be of practical help to pastoral leaders working to guide congregations in faithful discipleship.

To make use of this book, however, you will have to do practical thinking in your own ministry context. You need to do such thinking in relation to your own ministry context partly because I write out of my own life — the perspective of a white middle-class educated Lutheran pastor, husband, and father of two. You might be different in every way, and yet I hope what I write will cause you to ponder how God is calling *you* to faith as way of life. In addition, you'll need to think along with me, because I didn't write a book to provide answers. Instead, the book clearly identifies the endemic problems pastoral leaders face in modeling and mediating Christian faith as a whole, lived daily. This book, then, casts a vision of pastoral leadership centered on the ability to shape persons and communities for living God-given faith.

Faith as a Way of Life

The Christian faith is a way of life lived in response to Jesus' invitation to "follow me" (Mark 8:34). The life of faith lived in response to Jesus' invitation — and the leadership called to guide and foster faithful lives — follows a basic pattern. That pattern is one of gathering and scattering: gathered into the life of God in Christ through the power of the Spirit and scattered for the sake of witness and service in daily life. In an era when many churches focus almost exclusively on gathering, the reassertion of this pattern has real power.

Yet simply pointing to a fundamental pattern of gathering and scattering is not enough to say how faith comes in the first place through God's work in Christ through the Holy Spirit. The gift of faith and the life it entails come by God's action for us through the life, death, and resurrection of Jesus Christ. By offering Jesus for us, God takes away the sin that separates us from God and offers us new life "in Christ." It is through this crucial transaction at the heart of the story of God's dealing with the world that faith comes to us — unexpected and undeserved. While many passages of Scripture speak to this core reality of our incorporation into God's work in Christ, St. Paul's letter to the Romans captures the dynamic succinctly: "Do you not know that all of us who have been baptized into Christ Jesus were baptized into his death? We were buried therefore with him by baptism into death, so

3

that as Christ was raised from the dead by the glory of the Father, we too might walk in newness of life" (Romans 6:3-4). Faith comes to us, Paul argues, by dying to sin and rising with Christ to new life.

Christian faith cannot simply be summed up in the dying and rising that makes us Christ's own. Too often, such core Christian ideas are turned into beliefs thought to encapsulate the core of Christianity. Yet Christian faith is not merely a set of beliefs about God, Jesus, baptism, or new life. No, Christian faith is a gift of God that entails dying to one way of life and rising to another lived not for ourselves, but for God. To receive Christian faith is, in St. Paul's words, "to walk in newness of life" (Romans 6:4). Paul shows that Christian faith is not simply a state of mind or a belief that has no practical consequences for daily living. Rather, it is a way of life marked by the mysterious union with Christ described by Paul in these words: "it is no longer I who live, but Christ who lives in me" (Galatians 2:20).

Christian faith, then, is God's gift, not just of salvation and new life, but of a whole new way of life "in Christ." Yet in order to get the whole picture, we must go one step further. Faith as a way of life is not given simply that we might be at one with God, assured of our special place in cosmic history. No, God's saving gift of faith shapes daily life lived in and for the sake of God's reconciling work in the world. Yale theologian Miroslav Volf argues that "the core task of pastoral leadership today — and a signal mark of its excellence — is the task of shaping persons and communities for living faith as a way of life in the world."[1] Christian discipleship, and the life of the Christian ministry that serves such discipleship, is, as Volf so plainly states, a way of life not for its own sake, as if sectarian purity were the goal, but *for the sake of the world.* Such a claim brings us back to the idea that life lived in response to Jesus' call is shaped according to a basic pattern: gathering in worship before God and scattering in witness and service for the sake of the world.

---

1. Shortly after receiving word of the funding of his proposal for this project, Miroslav Volf wrote a short article on the themes of the project. See Miroslav Volf, "Way of Life," *Christian Century,* November 20, 2002, http://www.findarticles.com/p/articles/mi_m1058/is_24_119/ai_95206022. Accessed March 10, 2007.

Christian ministry is deeply concerned with proclaiming the transforming power of God's gift of faith in the daily lives of disciples. Pastors will be able to impart this vision of faith only if they themselves are compelled by it and if their parishioners find that the model helps them make sense of life as a whole. One of the most pressing needs of pastoral ministry is to develop, sustain, and legitimize reflection on Christian faith not simply as a set of propositions to believe, commandments to obey, or rituals to perform, but as an orienting force that impacts every aspect of daily life.

The Project behind This Book

Generously supported by Lilly Endowment, Inc., as part of the Sustaining Pastoral Excellence Program, the Faith as a Way of Life Project was designed to address the problems and prospects regarding pastoral leadership for the life of faith. A working group of pastors, laity, and theological educators met over a period of three years. In a series of reflective retreats, we tried to uncover both the problems with, and the possibilities for, pastoral leadership that models and mediates faith as a way of life.

A Few Terms Defined

Some comment on a few key terms is in order. The term "pastoral leadership" is used consistently throughout this book for two reasons. First, it is a way to focus on the church's great task of ministry in and for the sake of the world. That is, the term (with echoes in the Vatican II statement "Pastoral Constitution on the Church in the Modern World," *Gaudium et Spes*)[2] seeks to describe the church's pastoral role

---

2. *Gaudium et Spes*, Promulgated by His Holiness Pope Paul VI on December 7, 1965. See http://www.vatican.va/archive/hist_councils/ii_vatican_council/documents/vat-ii_cons_19651207_gaudium-et-spes_en.html. Accessed on February 23, 2007.

in relationship to faith lived out in the world. All Christians fulfill this role as members of the church, living out their callings in the world. It is a special role of pastoral leadership in the church to foster, equip, and encourage faith as a way of life. Second, "pastoral leader" is one term that helps deal with the great diversity of kinds of formal church leadership, not all of which even fit under the fairly general rubric of "clergy."

The term "excellence" might feel strange to some in relation to the life of the church and to pastoral leadership particularly. "Excellence," a buzzword in business circles, offers a way to point to marks of quality. Yet excellence in the context of corporate life raises concerns because of its focus on growth, efficiency, and avoidance of vulnerability. Ministry has its own measure of growth, which may best be accomplished through rather inefficient means and an embrace of vulnerability. Thus, while desiring to uphold a vision of excellence, Jackson Carroll argues that a term such as "excellence" must be placed "within the horizon of God's saving work in Jesus' life, death, and resurrection" in order for it to be fully useful to the church.[3]

Working Together over Three Years

The twenty-five members of the project's working group represented diverse regions of the country and traditions within the Christian church. As we met twice a year over three years we explored from as many vantage points as possible one central mark of excellent ministry: the call to proclaim God's transforming power to shape persons and communities for faith as a way of life.[4] We came to believe that the most effective way to find traction on the idea of living faith in all

3. Jackson Carroll, *God's Potters: Pastoral Leadership and the Shaping of Congregations* (Grand Rapids: Eerdmans, 2006), 194-218.

4. Jackson Carroll's important study of pastoral leadership in the United States is framed in terms of excellence in the core task of "shaping communities"; he does not as clearly highlight our focus here: that the shaping is for living faith as a way of life for the sake of the world. See *God's Potters*.

spheres of life was through theological reflection — itself a difficult practice that surprisingly did not come naturally to us. By theological reflection, I mean the practice of moving through a reflective circle beginning within God's active presence in the midst of a community of faith. This reflective circle entails an examination of the realities confronting us, engagement with biblical and theological resources to envision a response, and enacting strategies that lead us back into our realities with hope of change.[5]

Yet in actual fact, our capacity to practice theological discernment lags behind its importance for living faithful lives today. It became clear in this project how hard it is, even for theologically trained pastors, to sustain practical theological reflection together. Too often our conversations quickly and predictably settled into the ruts of the "primary languages" of American culture — what amount to a mixture of feelings, experience, and pragmatism, without reference to faith's conviction rooted in scripture.[6]

All of us, pastoral leaders included, can revert to other powerful languages to orient our work while covering it with a veneer of faith language. Clergy are often attracted to the emotion-driven therapeutic and the results-driven managerial models of leadership so prevalent in American culture. Caring deeply about how people feel and pressing for measurable congregationals growth are often highly rewarded skills among clergy. Yet when they dominate, faith becomes a weak sibling, doing little work as a community enacts its faith in daily life. Many excellent clergy in some measure understand this, and they long to grow in their ability to model and mediate a strong and comprehensive vision of Christian faith in relation to contemporary cultures. I hope this book can be of help.

---

5. This movement — often called the "hermeneutical circle" — can be traced back to the philosopher Hans-Georg Gadamer, *Truth and Method, Second Revised Edition* (New York: Continuum, 1989) and is common to many proposals regarding practical theology, as in Don Browning, *Towards a Fundamental Practical Theology: Descriptive and Strategic Proposals* (Minneapolis: Fortress Press, 1991).

6. I spell out in more detail what I mean by "primary languages" in Chapter Three below.

What you will read in these pages draws inspiration from the work of the Faith as a Way of Life Project, and under the voice of one author it tries to proclaim for the church more broadly some of what we learned. In that sense, what I say here is greatly indebted to the group and the work we shared. Yet I have imposed my own ideas and given shape to the argument in ways that both reflect the broader group discussions and seek to go beyond them.

The breadth of the topic is appropriate for a book on pastoral leadership in that its concerns are of the "generalist" sort rather than the "specialist" literature common in many fields. Seeking to write about faith as a way of life, let alone trying to live it and offer help to others on their journey, necessarily means wading into areas where I am not an expert. In a sense, the generalist — as I consider myself here — must be willing to be corrected by the specialist in many areas for the sake of asking the specialist to see the interconnection and coherence of the whole. I know the corrections will come, but we need to begin the discussion nonetheless.

Outline of the Book

This book has three main parts that work together in sequential fashion. The first part attempts a sketch of the major structural and cultural forces that account for the constrained role faith and the church play in the lives of many people today. The second part, while certainly not exhaustive, moves through some of the central aspects — or spheres, as I call them — of our lives. Finally, in part three, I sketch a vision of pastoral leadership for faith as way of life.

The middle section is really the heart of the book. These chapters are an attempt to think theologically about various spheres of life (such as family, work, politics, and the arts) that we often experience as fragmented and disconnected from one another. It is my belief affirmed concretely during my three years learning with the Faith as a Way of Life (FWL) national working group, that theological reflection is crucial to a full understanding of pastoral excellence. By encouraging the practical skill of thinking theologically about everyday matters, I hope to aid pastoral leaders (and those to whom they minister) in the task of living faithfully in the world.

Each of these sphere-focused chapters follows a similar pattern. Each deals with one of the distinct spheres of our society (and of our lives), and in each, I offer a three-part process of reflection. First, I highlight how the social-structural and cultural realities discussed in part one of the book come to bear within that sphere. Second, I propose some biblical and theological resources that portray how God acts to transform our lives so that faith can impact the realities pulling us apart. Third, drawing on pastoral leaders who were part of our project, I offer examples of pastoral leadership and Christian practice.

A note on reading: if you are most of all concerned about the practical "how-to" of engaging with God's gathering and scattering, you might begin with part two of the book. Do not take this as permission to skip part one, however. Early readers have said that part one is more difficult, but rewarding in the way that climbing a mountain is rewarding — it offers a clear view of the surrounding terrain. You might even begin by reading chapters one and eight to get a sense of the whole book before taking up parts one and two — the real substance of the book.

This brief book takes on nothing less than how Christians might more fully participate in the great mission of God always already at work in the world. Such a big topic, done in a few pages, necessarily means I often paint with broad brushstrokes. A final word, then, by way of introduction: I encourage you to see this work not as concluding a conversation but as provoking one. Whoever you are, I encourage you to think, to pray, and to seek more resources for a conversation with others who care deeply about the character and faithfulness of our life in Christ. We have developed a website partner to this book with many additional resources.[7] You can turn there for theological readings, sample sermons, adult and youth education plans, graphics and art, poetry, and more.

7. Go to www.yale.edu/faith/fwl.

Faith as a way of life is not a "new" model of pastoral leadership that requires you to attend seminars for training. Rather, it is an attempt to clear away the obstacles that prevent us from seeing the height and depth and breadth of God's gift of grace and mercy in Christ Jesus that by the power of the Spirit turns us from death to life. Such turning from death to life gives us our task: exercising the faith given to us as disciples and as leaders, shaping communities of discipleship living our faith as a way of life in and for the sake of the world.

PART ONE

Obstacles to Faith as a Way of Life

Let me make the assumption that you are in agreement that pastoral excellence centers on the ability to shape persons and communities for living faith as a way of life. Can one say with confidence that this vision is widely shared? And even if it were, could it be said that such ability among pastoral leadership is everywhere a reality? Do Christians practice faith as a way of life, and do pastoral leaders foster it in communities they lead? If research on pastoral leadership is any indication, then we can safely say that the core work of pastoral leadership is itself considered one of the major difficulties in ministry today. In reporting on massive survey data gathered by the Pulpit and Pew Project at Duke University, Jackson Carroll writes, "We asked pastors about a number of daily problems they face; the one that they reported as their greatest challenge was reaching people with the gospel in today's world. Seventy-four percent overall said that this was a problem they faced on a day-to-day basis."[1]

What he means, of course, is that many people today find the world's fast-paced changes confusing, and as a result they struggle to know how to speak about living the Christian faith today. The challenge to bring the gospel message — the same yesterday, today, and tomorrow (Hebrews 13:8) — to a world convulsed by dramatic changes

1. Jackson Carroll, *God's Potters: Pastoral Leadership and the Shaping of Congregations* (Grand Rapids: Eerdmans, 2006), 32.

is a challenge for anyone. While the question from the Pulpit and Pew survey does not use the same language as "faith as a way of life," it nonetheless fits within the basic orientation this book seeks to hold up for reflection. And to hear that three quarters of pastors say this task is a problem points to the profound need for the resources this book seeks to offer.

What, then, are the major obstacles in today's world that make difficult "reaching people with the gospel," to quote Jackson Carroll's question — in other words, modeling and mediating faith as a way of life? Carroll offers a discussion of social and cultural characteristics of our contemporary context that impact the work of ministry: broad demographic changes, increasing religious diversity, growing religious conflict, the impact of consumerism and choice, and the congregational bias in American religious life. While some of these points are obvious, understanding others may require you to read *God's Potters,* a book very much worth reading. But I want to step away from the "laundry list" approach Carroll takes to show social and cultural characteristics that prove to be durable and substantial obstacles to the life of discipleship and the ministry that serves to shape and encourage it.

By stepping back and focusing on two main obstacles, one each in the following two chapters, I hope to show both how durable these obstacles are and how difficult excellent pastoral leadership is in response. While this does not excuse what Greg Jones and Kevin Armstrong call "mediocrity masquerading as faithfulness," it does help diligent pastors and the congregations they serve to understand more deeply why they struggle, and sometimes fail, in the effort to do what they think matters most.[2] Let me restate the point: While some pastoral leaders may suffer from the ancient sin of sloth, a majority of them seek to do their work faithfully and well, yet struggle to do so exactly because of the ways they and their congregants are caught within the force field of broad and durable social and cultural obstacles.

2. L. Gregory Jones and Kevin R. Armstrong, *Resurrecting Excellence: Shaping Faithful Christian Ministry* (Grand Rapids: Eerdmans, 2006), 2.

I call the two obstacles the problems of compartmentalization and self-maximization.[3] While the first has roots in changes in the social structure of our society and the other relates to powerful cultural traditions, both shape us and therefore impact our minds, our hearts, and our actions. While I highlight their basic shape in the next two chapters, in various ways they will be woven throughout the whole book. These two forces shape us far more than we want to admit.

3. Miroslav Volf describes similar obstacles in outlining "The Church's Great Malfunctions," *Christianity Today*, http://www.christianitytoday.com/ct/2006/october/52.108.html (accessed March 12, 2007). Here Volf describes two malfunctions of faith — both faith's idleness, to which the obstacles I discuss contribute powerfully, and also faith's oppressiveness, the use of faith to justify violence. I ought to note that while I don't deal with faith's oppressiveness in depth, many people in our society today may object exactly to the main point of this book — God's call to live faith as a way of life — as by definition an example of the oppressiveness of faith. This is so because they view religion as irrational and dangerous when it does not remain, as the typical liberal argument goes, private and personal. For a best-selling example of such a critique, see Sam Harris, *The End of Faith: Religion, Terror, and the Future of Reason* (New York: W. W. Norton, 2004).

CHAPTER TWO

Life, Compartmentalized

"You can't worship two gods at once. Loving one god, you'll end up hating the other. Adoration of one feeds contempt for the other. You can't worship God and Money both."

Matthew 6:24 *(The Message)*

There is another side to Liz's comment at coffee hour that Sunday after worship. When she ribbed me about how I "think about this religion stuff all the time," she began with the exclamation, "I don't know how you do it!" There was a hint of longing there, as if somehow because of my career I could have singleness of focus and an integrated life. In her view, I had solved the struggle she feels as multiple voices within her soul and in her daily life compete with one another for her time. From many other conversations on other days, I knew that she felt pulled in various directions and never felt like any aspect of her life got its due. While this feeling of disconnection, of living a compartmentalized life, is simply a result of the structure of modern society, many find it very distressing. Knowing some measure of peace through participation in worship, Liz expressed through her joking a hope for something more coherent.

Where did the feeling of disconnection Liz expressed come from? Sociologist Robert Bellah, an astute analyst of modern American society, describes it this way:

It is often said that people today find themselves "fragmented and exhausted." We rush from work to family to school to recreation to church, if there is time for church, shifting gears and changing personalities, it would almost seem, each time we move from one context to another. . . . [W]e jump into our cars and rush from one impersonal location to another, always hoping we can find a little solace at the end of the day at "home." But at home most of us spend several hours in front of a television set watching things jump around from drama to comedy to sports, always interrupted by incessant advertisements, in a way even more chaotic than the rest of our lives.[1]

Bellah points to the way our lives are caught between various competing parts of daily life. Religion is at best one piece of a busy life, perhaps impacting one's "soul" or "heart" as a means to help cope with the hectic pace of the rest of life, where other values rule.

The issue clearly goes deeper than simply fragmentation of our lives. It goes deeper exactly at the point where Bellah, in the quote above, imagines "shifting gears and changing personalities . . . each time we move from one context to another." The core problem is that the spheres of modern life have semi-independence, each operating according to its own logic and values. Because we each live in and through them all, we internalize the value conflicts between them and compartmentalize as a mechanism for surviving the tensions. Faith has its own tidy sphere on Sundays and in one's soul, but the spheres of work, family, politics, and the arts are each oriented by their own values that usurp the proper place of faith in shaping our thought and action. In such a vision of modern life, love of neighbor may rule the soul, but love of a bargain rules in shopping, love of taste and beauty rules in the arts, and so on. In giving our allegiance to these various sphere-centered values, we in a sense make them gods — each the source of ultimate value within its sphere. In such circumstances, we

1. Robert N. Bellah, "Max Weber and World-Denying Love: A Look at the Historical Sociology of Religion," *Journal of the American Academy of Religion* 67/2: 279-80.

face the question German sociologist Max Weber asked about living in the modern world: "Which of the warring gods should we serve?"[2]

We're All Polytheists Now

The problem of modern polytheism arises, argued Weber, when one looks at the contrast between the social structure in ancient agrarian societies and the social structure of the modern societies. Weber argues that ancient societies were largely coordinated in all aspects of life through kinship networks and neighborly reciprocity. No independent sphere of "politics," "religion," or "economics" existed; all were intertwined within the daily life and the immediate needs of the people. In contrast, Weber argued, modern society has developed various distinct and competing spheres, each oriented to its own values and increasingly in conflict with fundamental religious convictions.

The origin of this dramatic conflict between "religious ethics" and the "values of the world," Weber argues, lies in the rise of prophets. Prophets introduced a sharp critique of agrarian societies in favor of what Weber called an "otherworldly ethic" given for the community by God. For example, the role of the commandments or teachings given by God through Moses or Jesus worked "to systematize and rationalize the way of life, either in particular points, or totally."[3] Whereas in early social forms the realm of the spiritual and the material are more or less continuous, the introduction of prophetic religion marks a sharp break between the two. In place of a holistic and continuous sphere of social life, including religious life, transcendent truth interrupts, calling believers out of the world for the sake of life lived according to transcendent values.[4]

2. Max Weber, "Science as a Vocation," 153, in *From Max Weber: Essays in Sociology*, trans. and ed. H. H. Gerth and C. Wright Mills (New York: Oxford University Press, 1946).

3. Max Weber, "Religious Rejections of the World and Their Directions," 327, in Gerth and Mills, *From Max Weber*.

4. In addition to Weber, "Religious Rejections," see also the important discussion in

How does this calling "deny" the world, and how does this matter to the development of social order? Because of the prophetic impulse, Weber argues, a rationalizing tendency emerges that first makes explicit a religious sphere separate from other elements of social life but eventually also impacts the development of other spheres of social life as well. The basic impulse of prophetic religion leads to the formation of its own community, oriented by communion with God and a related "objectless world denying love."[5] It is world denying because it denies the particular worldly values — familial love, economic reciprocity, or civic duty.

Thus a distinct religious sphere emerges that is in some tension with the former organizing values within various spheres. While the demanding prophetic impulse explicitly offered an ethic for living within each sphere of life, its radical departure from the ordinary "worldly" values created two options: follow the radical precepts of prophetic religion, or seek in response to find other means within the bounds of worldly spheres of life to account for their organization in a sense "on their own." In other words, then, the "do unto your neighbor as your neighbor does unto you" as a communal ethic separates from religious justification to become more distinct as an inter-communal economic value. This process of differentiation, Weber thought, becomes "wider the more the values of the world have been rationalized and sublimated in terms of their own laws."[6]

These "rationalizing potentialities" existed in many civilizations but went through a dramatic development in Western society, leading to the breakthrough to modernity, or what Weber often simply called "capitalism."[7] Here, Weber attempted to account for the remarkable rise in economic might in the nations of Western Europe. What could account for such a remarkable thing as the industrial revolution, an unprecedented period of productivity, innovation and wealth creation?

Robert Bellah, "Religious Evolution," in Robert N. Bellah and Steven M. Tipton, *The Robert Bellah Reader* (Durham: Duke University Press, 2006), esp. 33-40.

5. Weber, "Religious Rejections," 329.

6. Weber, "Religious Rejections," 330.

7. Robert Bellah, "Max Weber and World-Denying Love," 280-81.

He pinpointed the Protestant Ethic, a Puritan understanding that while one's ultimate salvation could never be absolutely sure, material gain showed divine blessing and was evidence of God's election.[8]

The Protestant Ethic spurred rationalization of the economy, according to Weber, and as this ethic increasingly became disconnected from pious intentions, only the profit motive remained. Rationalization occurred not only in the economy, but also in government, the arts, and other spheres of society, so that these main spheres of life became gradually separated from religious values that oriented their actions, with the result that in these spheres other ultimate values came to dominate.[9]

While Weber greatly admired the prophetic impulse and its coherent ethic of life, he saw how its severity meant that only those whom he called "virtuosi" such as St. Francis actually lived it. Instead, historic developments that included the rationalization and secularization of the economic, political, aesthetic, and other spheres meant a greatly reduced sphere of influence for prophetic religion. In this sphere, perhaps, the call of the God of the Jews and Christians still inspired people to live according to the main value of prophetic religion — in Weber's rather technical term, *acosmic,* or world-denying, love. As opposed to worldly love, that is, the love we have for particular people, places or things, Weber is here referring to the call to love as God loves — without distinction, including friends, strangers and even enemies.[10] Yet the reduced sphere of influence of this radical religious impulse to love unconditionally caused Weber great worry exactly because such a reduction meant historical developments leading to what he called "modern polytheism." Why would this be worrisome? Through living in each sphere, society produces

8. See what is perhaps his most famous work: Max Weber, *The Protestant Ethic and the Spirit of Capitalism* (New York: Charles Scribner's Sons, 1958).

9. Perhaps the most important development of this aspect of Weber's theory is Jürgen Habermas's magisterial two-volume *The Theory of Communicative Action* (Boston: Beacon Press, 1984-87), in which he uses the framework of "systems and lifeworld" to describe the increasing colonization of the realms of the lifeworld by the systems of economic and state power.

10. See Bellah, "Max Weber and World-Denying Love," 277-78.

within us a moral pluralism that allows us to move through the spheres of our lives enacting the appropriate value-set demanded by the "gods" of that sphere of life.[11]

Spheres of Life: Examples

Kinship

Kinship marks the first sphere in Weber's discussion in large part because he views it as the elemental sphere out of which the others evolved. Archaic societies were organized according to two "elemental principles: first, the dualism of in-group and out-group morality; second, for in-group morality, simple reciprocity: 'As you do unto me I shall do unto you.'"[12] Such elemental principles contained the basic pattern of social kinship and economic networks, along with connected traditions of magic and natural religion. Within such kinship networks, regardless of status, an obligation to trade, and even freely give, resources followed the logic of "your want of today may be mine of tomorrow." While these open channels of gift exchange existed within the clan or tribe, they did not cross over to other groups. Outsiders were treated according to separate codes of behavior. For example, while internally those who had plenty were responsible to offer special aid to those in need within the community, outsiders whose resources failed could be made slaves.

The intervention of prophetic religion into archaic society made its first and perhaps most profound impact here. Weber gives Jesus as his example when he claims that for prophetic religion, "those who cannot be hostile to members of the household, to father and to mother, cannot be disciples of Jesus."[13] The "call" of "salvation religion" asks for primary allegiance to the savior over natural allegiance to personal

11. Weber, "Religious Rejections," 323-59.
12. Weber, "Religious Rejections," 329.
13. Weber, "Religious Rejections," 329.

relations: mother and father, husband or wife, and wider circles of kin. Primary allegiance means, positively, "love of the neighbor/stranger whom I do not know as I love myself."

Through this shift in allegiance, the ethic of the kinship community is transferred to the congregation. According to Robert Bellah, "what has happened to the two principles of the ancient ethic of neighborliness is that the principle of the contrast between in-group and out-group has been abandoned and the principle of reciprocity has been absolutized."[14] Or, going beyond Bellah, one might say that the principle of simple kinship reciprocity has been transformed by God's intervention into a principle of generosity — giving regardless, even to enemies.[15] Weber has exactly such a transformation to a principle of radical generosity in mind when he writes of the religious person "being 'moved' and edified to feeling a direct communion with God," communion that "always inclined men towards the flowing out into an objectless acosmism of love."[16] He continues that while the particulars of this love vary across history and within specific religious traditions, it almost always "goes beyond all barriers of societal associations, often including that of one's own faith."[17] The fact, then, is that particular loyalty to kinship, or natural relations of any sort, clash loudly with the kind of otherworldly love that prophetic religion demands — a love released from its 'natural' ties for the sake of a radical love of all without regard. I shall explore this further in relation to contemporary family life in chapter four below. Already, however, the wrenching demand of Jesus to "follow me" comes rushing to the foreground and leaves little space for a naïve view that Christians are simply called to love our husbands or wives and, together, love our children.[18]

---

14. Bellah, "Max Weber and World-Denying Love," 283.

15. My thanks to Miroslav Volf for this point.

16. This odd phrase, *liebsakosmismus,* is a combination of *akosmismus,* world-denial, and *liebe,* love. Bellah discusses the term, and its use by Weber, at great length in "Max Weber and World-Denying Love," 286-92.

17. Weber, "Religious Rejections," 330.

18. One finds this rhetoric especially common in popular literature by such groups as Focus on the Family, Concerned Women of America, and other conservative groups.

Economy

The connections between the sphere of kinship and the sphere of the economy are plain. As in the sphere of kinship, Weber begins by showing how in ancient societies tension did not exist between religion and economy. In a sense, religion served efforts to attain material security, including health, children, food, and perhaps some extra for lean times. Yet as markets developed, the barter economy gave way to a more rational economy based on money. Money, as Weber says, is "the most abstract and 'impersonal' element that exists in human life."[19] The more the market turns towards internal laws of profit and interest through money as an abstract calculation of value, the less it fits with any prophetic impulse that in God's name aims to treat all equally. Why is this so? In a money economy, personal relationships do not exist, or if they do, they are not determinative. Other factors drive economic growth, including calculations regarding prices that simply do not take account of the value of persons in and of themselves.

Therefore, when in the world of work profit is the highest value, or serves as its "god," persons serve the end of profit. Such a system will think of people as exchangeable pieces of labor to be applied to material in the production process. Such an understanding helps make sense of the oft-repeated quote from Henry Ford: "Why do I always get the whole person when all I really need is a pair of hands?" In such a rationalized system, Weber worried, human beings would become trapped in an economic system characterized by "specialists without spirit."[20] I'll contrast this reductive view of human life and labor to a more robust theology of work in chapter five below. Yet even short of spelling out a Christian view of work, it is clear that such an understanding of value in relation to economy sacrifices human good at the altar of profit.

19. Weber, "Religious Rejections," 331.
20. Weber, *The Protestant Ethic*, 182.

Politics

Tensions between religion and political aspects of early societies did not exist in the way we are considering in this chapter, despite the obvious social conflict that did exist between peoples. These early societies imagined that their gods were the protectors of their "locality, tribe, and polity" and were only "concerned with the interests of their respective associations."[21] While they might be called upon for support during conflict with other communities, they served everyday life in an integrated way as if they were — and sometimes they indeed were — literally part of the kinship networks. Prophetic religion drove a wedge between faith in God and archaic political society by introducing the idea of one God, whose nature was love of all people without regard for their kinship or ethnicity.

Weber describes the modern state, a development that took millennia to be sure, as substantially the same in its modes of operation as the sphere of modern economics. Political action is, finally, carried out through an impersonal imposition of rules, principles, and the law. Its orienting values are appropriate distributions of power for all people, so that the state cannot act with love — let alone the self-giving love called for in the heart of prophetic religion. In its internal administration, and especially with regard to foreign policy, the state legitimates its very existence by means of force. Weber puts the contrast at its starkest: "The Sermon on the Mount says 'resist no evil.' In opposition, the state asserts: 'You shall help right to triumph by the use of force, otherwise you too may be responsible for injustice.'"[22] While at least in some polities (democratic, for instance) consent of the governed and the ideals of founding documents (a constitution, for instance) act to legitimate state actions, ultimately force rules. Even in a democratic polity, however, the state that cannot safeguard its own existence with force is vulnerable to disintegration. Von Clausewitz fa-

21. Weber, "Religious Rejections," 333.
22. Weber, "Religious Rejections," 334.

mously argued as much when he wrote that "war is a continuation of politics by other means."[23]

While every sphere indeed offers "gods" that can claim our allegiance and orient our action, only a few actually offer a substitute to salvation. Weber, writing during World War I, saw this possibility with war — the extreme pole of politics' use of force. "Death on the field of battle," Weber wrote, "differs from . . . merely unavoidable dying in that in war, and in this massiveness only war, the individual can believe that he knows he is dying 'for' something."[24] When this happens, total commitment to the state is elevated to a pseudo-spiritual good, and those who die are rewarded with "immortality" of a sort through honoring heroic action with medals, parades, and later, monuments. Yet from the perspective of prophetic religion, following an absolute command, "Thou shall not kill," and "You shall love thy neighbor as thyself," such self-sacrifice for the sake of the nation must, Weber argues, "appear as a glorification of fratricide."[25]

Aesthetics

The sphere of the arts emerged in dynamic interaction with religious belief. From the earliest societies, art has expressed the imagination through drawings, music, dance, sculpture, and crafting of objects of all sorts from instruments to buildings and their furnishings. Yet with the rise of prophetic religion form is subjected to meaning. For example, the content of a painting such as Michelangelo's *The Creation of Adam* (1510) makes the painting valuable. Chardin's *The Silver Tumbler* (1766), however, represents the sort of aesthetic experiment in which a simple domestic scene becomes the vehicle to explore medium or form. This transition from Michelangelo to Chardin shows the transition to modern society, where art develops according to form

---

23. Carl von Clausewitz, *On War* (New York: Penguin Classics, 1983 [1832]).
24. Weber, "Religious Rejections," 335.
25. Weber, "Religious Rejections," 336.

and the logic of taste cut loose from substantive meaning in relation to ethics or religion. Art, to say it differently, no longer must express religious content but can be good simply as diversion, as a form that evokes a positive feeling (tasteful, rather than good in a moral sense). Understood solely as form, art is "without reasons" and therefore "irrational." As such, it provides a space of escape from the rationalizing spheres of politics and economy. It in a sense provides — through the "escape" of music, drama, story, painting, or another medium — an alternative "salvation from the routines of everyday life."[26]

While Weber goes on to treat further examples through discussions of the erotic and intellectual spheres, his analysis simply deepens in similar directions. His conclusion, finally, is that every sphere denies the love central to prophetic religion: the unconditional love of God, and the love of the neighbor as oneself. He describes the unbridled erotic drive as "veiled and sublimated brutality" because of its irrational seeking of pleasure for oneself through the other. And he describes the sphere of the intellect as ruled by an "aristocracy of the intellect" where the irrational claims of self-giving love finally have no defense. As Weber looked at modern society, he saw a life of fragmented and rationalized spheres in which little space exists for the orienting force of self-giving love to shape a way of life. "Under the technical and social conditions of rational culture," Weber concludes, "an imitation of the life of Buddha, Jesus, or Francis seems condemned to failure for purely external reasons."[27]

The Church and Its Pastoral Leadership

Max Weber, it seems, arrived at the dour position that there is "little room" for the practice of discipleship in the world. To a large extent, one could say, most churches and pastoral leaders have accepted the demotion to one sphere of life — that of things "spiritual." These

26. Weber, "Religious Rejections," 342.
27. Weber, "Religious Rejections," 357.

spiritual things happen in the heart and the church. Pastoral leaders therefore busy themselves with creating programs that will attract people to church — emotionally resonant music, compelling preaching, and programmatic offerings for youth and adults that fit with their age-graded concerns throughout the life course. In order to assure regular participation, they simply set up motivational systems for achieving attendance through initiatives such as "perfect attendance month" that work to reward the already highly committed and to scold the Easter/Christmas members who enjoy the fruits without contributing their labor.

What is lost in this vision of church? What is lost is the vision of gathering and scattering under the claim of the Lord of all creation. The church ceases to be a busy intersection, a nexus where disciples are equipped to be seed and light, salt and yeast, for the sake of the world God loves, both modeling an alternative ordering of life in the economics and politics of their gathering and living out such an alternative scattered among many worldly callings. Instead of this, the church as one sphere among many mostly bears out Weber's view that the radical claims of Jesus are for the heart and heaven. While people might be sent out into the world, it is only for bringing others into the life of the church, putting a claim on their hearts for heaven, offering a mystic escape from the rational ordering of work and the political sphere.

In the rough-and-tumble of government or business, we play by the rules of the game in that sphere or we get stepped on. The recent entrance of the Religious Right into American politics only proves the point: they have used faith as an entry into hardball politics. When the faith is politicized, political values usurp the guiding authority faith could properly have within the sphere of politics, thus reinforcing the conflict between spheres and the image of their mutual impermeability.

To return to my opening story about Liz, and her sense that I somehow had escaped the fragmentation she experienced in her life, I can say honestly that this is not so simply the case. While I do not wholly share Weber's brooding picture of the modern world, the difficulty of actually extending an acosmic love, a love of all "without regard," in modern society is a challenge that must necessarily take all the creativity and effort we have to offer. Robert Bellah, who is a realist but never the exemplary pessimist that Weber seems to have been, argues that we do have twentieth-century examples of acosmic love in the cases of large social movements led by Mohandas Gandhi and Martin Luther King Jr.[28] In their leadership, King and Gandhi exemplified the ethic of unconditional love with profound, if compromised, political and economic effect. Such social movements in civil society have also been a key component of Jürgen Habermas's argument that economic and political systems, now working according to their own internalized rationality, must be returned to an effective grounding in the "lifeworld" — his term for civil society, including home, church, and other civic organizations.[29] Such an effort to reground these systems in the lifeworld and its meaning-driven values would be a tremendously difficult task, but not to his mind an impossible one. Such an effort could not be accomplished once for all; rather the effort itself is a condition of our life in the modern world, and it will require offering, by vibrant pastoral leadership, another way to be in the world.

As the next chapter will show, however, too often the tactics taken up by the church and its pastoral leadership are already shaped by a culture of individualism that powerfully constrains the church's vision. The power of the cultural tradition of individualism so powerfully frames our way of thinking and acting that much of the church's leadership simply accepts its position within a single sphere of life, seeking to effectively manage its organization and care for those within its bounds. Clearly naming the constraints of a cultural tradition of individualism works hand in hand with seeing the logic of the warring spheres as we seek to clear a way towards effective pastoral leadership for faith to serve as an orienting force in all spheres of life.

28. Bellah, "Max Weber and World-Denying Love," 300.

29. Jürgen Habermas, *Theory of Communicative Action, Volume Two: Lifeworld and System;* see also Jean L. Cohen and Andrew Arato, *Civil Society and Political Theory* (Cambridge: MIT Press, 1992).

CHAPTER THREE

Lives, Self-Maximized

In this way we are like the various parts of a human body. Each part gets its meaning from the body as a whole, not the other way around. The body we're talking about is Christ's body of chosen people. Each of us finds our meaning and function as a part of his body.

Romans 12:4-5 *(The Message)*

Despite having some historical family ties to religious traditions, for the most part Liz viewed church as a consumer product whose value was calculated through cost-benefit analysis. Liz was a third-generation member of our Lutheran congregation. While she and her family lived in a nearby suburban community, they continued to drive to this church in a poor inner-city neighborhood out of a conviction that it would be good for their kids. Liz wanted them to have some connection to family heritage, to be sure, and in addition the kids would get a safe "cross-cultural" experience through the connection to a church in the city. As I grew to understand the calculations that drove their church involvement, I began to understand why their pattern of participation largely fit the school year (they never came to church during vacations from school save the Christmas Eve and Easter services). For Liz and her family, church — as they told me plenty of times — offered an hour of peace in the midst of their frenetic family life.

27

What sort of "peace" did they expect from their participation on Sunday mornings? I don't want to over-simplify a complicated faith shaped by many things. Further, I don't think it makes sense to simply say that her focus was wrong. To the contrary, she followed what Nancy Ammerman has called "Golden Rule Christianity" — a simple conviction that God loves us and wants us to help others. This simple faith is what drove her commitment to being in church at all.[1] However, such an understanding of Christian faith, common though it may be, is not very grounded in orthodox Christian practice and belief. It is a thin faith largely influenced by the dominant culture of American life, with little substance upon which one could build a critique of the competing worldly values examined in the previous chapter.[2] As this chapter seeks to make plain, a commitment to church — and an understanding of the faith itself — so deeply molded by the American tradition of individualism fundamentally distorts faith and weakens its power to orient daily living.

We're All Individualists Now

The problem remains that powerful American cultural traditions shape the way people in our culture talk about their lives. Whether called "personalism" or "individualism" of one sort or another, when such cultural traditions become a primary language, and faith a secondary language, we fall out of the practice of thinking and talking about our lives in ways that are explicitly shaped by faith. The con-

1. Nancy T. Ammerman, "Golden Rule Christianity: Lived Religion in the American Mainstream," in David Hall, ed., *Lived Religion in America* (Princeton: Princeton University Press, 1997), 196-216.

2. Drawing on and developing the ideas of Clifford Geertz and Michael Waltzer, Miroslav Volf had used the terms "thin" and "thick" religion in an important essay on "Christian and Violence." His point, which I depend on here, is that " 'thinning' of religious practice opens religious convictions to be misused to legitimize violence because it strips away precisely what in 'thick' religious faith guards against such misuse." See http://repository.upenn.edu/boardman/2/ (accessed February 25, 2007), 5.

verse is also true: the primary language of individualism reorients faith so that it too becomes merely personal — a conversation between Jesus and me — or worse, a calculation about how much I need to do for God in order to receive a blessing in my life.[3]

The power of a faith reduced by individualism not only shapes an "average" Christian like Liz, but also the church's pastoral leadership. The truth is that even pastors struggle to grasp faith as a whole and to have it "at hand" as a coherent vision of their own lives, let alone the life of the community they lead. In part, the trouble lies in the fragmented nature of theological education that gives prospective pastors a piecemeal collection of information on the Bible, theology, church history, and "the arts of ministry," and asks them to integrate this academic wisdom into the work of ministry largely on their own. This is, thankfully, beginning to change, as Charles Foster and his co-authors recently documented in *Educating Clergy,* their landmark study of seminary education in America.[4]

While theological education plays a contributing role, the core problem lies with the durable "common culture" of the United States and the strength of its primary cultural languages that shape our ways of living in the world. Too often, however, sociologists portray this influence in simplified fashion. Alan Wolfe's *The Transformation of American Religion: How We Actually Live Our Faith* presents this thesis: "In every aspect of the religious life, American faith has met American culture — and American culture has triumphed."[5] Christianity in America, Wolfe writes, tends to paint "a picture of religious believers as a people set apart — their eyes focused not on the

---

3. The common phrase in some churches, "When the praises go up, the blessings come down," ought to be criticized exactly at this point. To such a perspective on God's blessing, the biblical witness regarding God's mercy and blessing, giving rain to the just and the unjust alike, can only be seen as an offense. See Matthew 5:45; also Philip Yancey, *What's So Amazing about Grace* (Grand Rapids: Zondervan, 1997).

4. See Charles R. Foster et al., *Educating Clergy: Pastoral Imagination and Teaching Practices* (San Francisco: Jossey-Bass, 2006).

5. Alan Wolfe, *The Transformation of American Religion: How We Actually Live Our Faith* (New York: The Free Press, 2003), 3.

mundane world around them but on the judgment that awaits them." In fact, Wolfe argues, such a set-apart and God-fearing people are not to be found in America now — if they ever were. After reviewing twenty years of ethnographic research on American religious life, he summarizes the effect of a dominant culture of "indulgent" or "therapeutic" individualism on faith: "Americans revere a God who is anything but distant, inscrutable, or angry. They are more likely to honor a God to whom they can pray in their own, self-chosen way."[6] "The faithful in the United States," he finds, "are remarkably like everyone else."[7]

Such words, whatever truth they may contain, rub pastoral leaders the wrong way. They work hard, often seven days a week, in order to be faithful to God and to the congregations they lead. They may find it easy to reject Wolfe's conclusions as the cynical thinking of a nonbeliever worried about the adverse impact of religious conviction in public life.

Still, arguments similar to Wolfe's have been made from the earliest decades of our nation's history. Explicating such arguments helps to make more sense of the power of cultural languages — and why Wolfe is on track by pointing to the power of "therapeutic individualism" to describe how many Americans approach their faith.

America's Primary Cultural Language

In their classic study *Habits of the Heart: Individualism and Commitment in American Life,* Robert Bellah and his four colleagues describe a common moral vocabulary Americans — despite all their conflicts and differences — share as a "primary language."[8] They name our primary language "individualism," tracing its roots back through the intellectual influences of our founding fathers to the utilitarian philoso-

6. Wolfe, *Transformation of American Religion,* 10.

7. Wolfe, *Transformation of American Religion,* 3.

8. Robert N. Bellah et al., *Habits of the Heart: Individualism and Commitment in American Life* (Berkeley: University of California Press, 1996 [1985]), 20.

phies of Thomas Hobbes and especially John Locke. Hobbes and Locke, each in his own way, theorized that society is based on a contract that individuals enter into for the sake of protection and to advance their own self-interest. For Locke, whose influence on America is deep, the justification for such a social contract was the prior existence of property and the need for individual protection of private ownership.[9] Given the way such a tradition envisions government as the protector of individual rights of property ownership, it is no surprise that the state and market are the primary institutional carriers of this common culture.[10]

When Alexis de Tocqueville, a young French social philosopher, traveled through America in the 1830s surveying the shape of its new democratic society, he sought to gauge the interrelationship of these conflicting ideals. On the one hand, he saw the idea of the free citizen acting in and through political life for the common good of the nation. He thought that the local private citizen, pursuing the task of democratic self-governance, learns the importance of, and contributes to, vibrant civic life. Tocqueville argued for the central role of religion, which he called "the first of [Americans'] political institutions."[11] Religion received this designation because participation in congregations shaped "habits of the heart" constraining liberty into socially constructive channels.[12] On the other hand, he saw the ideal of liberty in pursuit of wealth and its pleasures. Here, he was among the first to use the term "individualism" as a means to describe the potential danger of liberty freed from social constraints. "Individualism," writes Tocqueville, "is a calm and considered feeling which disposes each citizen to isolate himself from the mass of his fellows and withdraw to a circle of family and friends; with his little society formed to his taste, he gladly leaves the greater society to look after

9. See especially John Locke, *Second Treatise of Government*.

10. Robert N. Bellah, "Is There a Common American Culture?" in Steven M. Tipton, *The Robert Bellah Reader* (Durham: Duke University Press, 2006), 322.

11. Alexis de Tocqueville, *Democracy in America*, ed. J. P. Mayer, trans. George Lawrence (New York: HarperPerennial, 1988 [1835, 1840]), 292.

12. Tocqueville, *Democracy in America*, 287.

itself."[13] While his trenchant foresight did describe the way market forces could produce a culture of consumer-oriented individuals disconnected from care for others, Tocqueville did not see how the language of faith offered a substantial alternative for shaping common life.

Writing a hundred and fifty years later, Robert Bellah and his colleagues found reason to worry about social corrosion and the overwhelming power of individualism in American life. Going beyond Tocqueville, however, their historical portrait of the United States highlights other cultural traditions — the republican and biblical traditions — that have shaped our nation and push back against the negative impact of individualism. Their research highlighted the institutional power of the state's focus on individual rights and the market focus on consumer choice as major shaping forces. As a result, Americans are gradually losing fluency with secondary languages that encourage community rather than individualism, self-giving rather than selfishness. To more carefully unpack the argument in *Habits of the Heart*, I'll briefly describe two types of individualism and the cultural characters — the *manager* and the *therapist* — that most distinctly embody each.

Individualism: Types and Characters

Each age has its symbols. One can easily call to mind images of the heroic founding fathers like Washington and Jefferson, the independent citizen-leaders from the colonial states whose labors shaped our nation. Just as easily, many can envision the great industrialists like Rockefeller or Carnegie who helped moved the nation from its agrarian origins into an urbanized and market-driven age. In speaking of representative types of individualism and the characters that fit hand-in-glove with those types, I am simply pointing to the ways social structure and culture interact in giving "living expression to a vision of life."[14] In Ameri-

13. Tocqueville, *Democracy in America*, 506.
14. Bellah et al., *Habits*, 39-40.

can society, we inescapably live in and through visions of life that shape and are shaped by these formative characters of each age. And these characters — like the founding fathers or the great industrialists — become "focal points" for contesting the values, hopes, and problems of a given moment in history.

Many important factors impacted the social evolution that has given rise to the social structure and culture of American society today. Few, however, compete with the durable and far-reaching impact of the rise of the business corporation and the welfare state. These patterns of bureaucratic organization are not unique to the United States, but they have developed in ways that have distinctly marked the shape of social life over the last generations. A key feature of this development, as I describe in the previous chapter, is a dramatic division of life into separate spheres — home and work, leisure and citizenship, and so on. Such compartmentalized life mirrors the organizing structure of bureaucracy with its various departments operating within a functional whole. It is not surprising that this new social structure would give rise to distinct forms of individualism — utilitarian and expressive — and the characters — the manager and the therapist — who have become symbols of our age.

Utilitarian Individualism

Utilitarian individualism, while rooted in the earliest days of the American republic, has been greatly strengthened as a cultural language in recent times, especially as a result of the power of the market economy. The utilitarian individual fundamentally sees human life in terms of the challenge to maximize self-interest. One might think of Benjamin Franklin as a founding contributor to such a vision for life. His *Poor Richard's Almanac* taught Americans a vocabulary for pursuing individual success by hard work and careful accounting. Aphorisms like "Early to bed, early to rise, makes a man healthy, wealthy and wise," or the classic "God helps those who help themselves," are such common coin in our culture that many even believe them to be biblical.[15] In a sense they are the sacred scripture of our culture.

Today, the life course of many Americans is so profoundly captive to this utilitarian individualist vision that it is almost impossible for many to think in other terms. The American dream has become a consumer dream of accumulation — of status, money, and material things. Individuals sacrifice, work hard, and play by the rules to get ahead. Within this mode of individualism it is the resonant character of the manager that looms large in American life — in business, to be sure, but as I will argue later, within non-profits and churches no less than in the private sector. [16]

The Manager

While the celebrity culture we live in might suggest that the media star or business entrepreneur would be the key character for our age, it is actually the person behind each of these "extraordinary" figures that is the real character to attend to here. Modern corporations, and the managers that run them, are the mainstay of modern American culture despite the perpetual fascination with prominent people such as Britney Spears or Bill Gates. The essence of the role of the manager, according to Robert Bellah and his co-authors, is "to organize the human and non-human resources available to the organization that employs him [or her] so as to improve its position in the marketplace."[17] The manager's role is to use technical knowledge, psychology, organizational insights, and sheer force of personality so that the organization meets the expectations of those in control — ultimately, the owners. The manager is, then, held either to the standard of market share (as in for-profit companies) or bureaucratic rules of performance (as in governmental agencies). Despite the need of the manager to deal with

15. Bellah et al., *Habits,* 32-33.
16. Alasdair MacIntyre, *After Virtue: A Study in Moral Theory,* 2nd ed. (Notre Dame: University of Notre Dame Press, 1984).
17. Bellah et al., *Habits,* 45.

interpersonal issues, even managing emotions, the manager is evaluated based on a calculation of effectiveness, that is, the success of the organization within its market sector.[18]

Expressive Individualism

Expressive individualism emerged as a romantic reaction against what was seen as a narrowly constrained life focused on work and wealth rather than a deeper cultivation of the self in its fullest capacities. Expressive — also interchangeably called therapeutic — individualism privileges "a unique core of feeling and intuition inside every person that should unfold or be expressed if individuality is to be realized."[19] Rather than the calculating image, this version of individualism sees human life as the task of expressing each person's unique feelings and inner being. Various features of American arts and letters embody this tradition, but perhaps none so robustly as the poet Walt Whitman. Spending his life in pursuit of poetry and the pleasures of living, he never achieved the kind of financial stability that allowed Franklin to retire mid-life. Yet Whitman's life became another measure of success — that of rich experience "open to all kinds of people, luxuriating in the sensual as well as intellectual, above all a life of strong feeling."[20]

In their interviews with Americans in the late twentieth century, Bellah and his research team found an important and widespread shift in the mode of commitments people make: from conscientiously choosing to live and act in ways that are "good in themselves" to choosing freely to do or experience something "because I like it." While in some sense in tension with the utilitarian model of life, the expressive individual still pursues self-maximization. Rather than measuring the value of choices based on utility, the expressive individ-

18. The classic discussion of management and emotional work is Arlie Hochschild, *The Managed Heart: The Commercialization of Human Feeling* (Berkeley: University of California Press, 2003 [1983]).

19. Bellah et al., *Habits,* 33-35, 334.

20. Bellah et al., *Habits,* 34.

ualist judges choices based on feeling or sentiment. Contemporary culture is equally comfortable in this mode, shifting from arguments about "what works" to assertions of "what I like" without pause.

The Therapist

The utilitarian and expressive modes have evolved together and depend on one another. So, therefore, it makes sense that the utilitarian mode's character, the manager, has its partner in the expressive mode. The *therapist* as a character type points to the life outside the realm of work and civic life where the manager holds sway. As the world of work has become geographically separated from personal life (family, community, church, etc.), a crisis of meaning arises as people ask about the meaning of their lives, besides being cogs in a well-managed machine. Enter the therapist, whose role is to improve personal satisfaction and meaning in life. In this mode, then, the therapist is also a technical expert alongside the manager, "a specialist in mobilizing resources for effective action." But here is the key difference: for the therapist "the resources are largely internal to the individual and the measure of effectiveness is the elusive criterion of personal satisfaction."[21] The therapist as a character type, therefore, offers a vision for life in which all commitments are chosen as means to enhance or develop the self and its life-satisfaction.

The Church and Its Pastoral Leadership

Bellah and his colleagues paint a bleak picture for the church as it seeks to embody something like the vision of communal life "in Christ" described by St. Paul (Romans 12:5). Consumer capitalism and its partner, the media, have fostered a common culture and vision of life centered on individuals making a life that feels good to them, find-

21. Bellah et al., *Habits,* 47.

ing satisfaction through whatever means are available.[22] In such a society, the characters of the manager and therapist "urge a strenuous effort to make our particular segment of life a small world of its own," shaped to the taste and pleasure of each individual.[23] Exactly here the primary language of individualism has an affinity with the division of life into spheres noted above, producing self-understanding stripped of normative social values and the constraints and responsibilities associated with community.

Religious life has inevitably been deeply influenced by this dominant cultural vision of life, and we all to a greater or lesser extent speak of our lives in the language of individualism. Historically American churches have been a central site of communal concern and public engagement. Yet various research shows that cultural shifts in the twentieth century — including not only the rise and dominance of bureaucratic organizations but also the unleashing of a "culture of choice" emerging from the upheavals of the 1960s — present new challenges to congregations.[24] In response to consumer pressures, churches are tempted to become intimate and privatized havens of personal solace and spiritual connection while neglecting deeper convictions regarding communal belonging and responsibility, in whatever form they might take within this or that denomination or tradition.

The resulting dominant model of religious participation embraces one's own little circle of shared style and taste while under-valuing life scattered to participate and impact the world for good. Bellah and his co-authors captured an extreme case of such religious privatization most memorably in their report on interviews with a woman named Sheila Larson. While she believes in God, she does not attend church and follows the guidance of her own religion, which she calls

22. Bellah argues that "there is an enormously powerful common culture in America and it is carried predominantly by the market and the state and by their agencies of socialization: television and education." Bellah, "Is There a Common American Culture?" 321.

23. Bellah et al., *Habits*, 50.

24. Philip Hammond, *Religion and Personal Autonomy: The Third Disestablishment in America* (Columbia: University of South Carolina Press, 1992).

"Sheilaism." "Sheilaism," it turns out, consists of "her own little voice" shorn of any objective or institutional grounding whatsoever.[25] Among other things, what worries Bellah and the others in this example of extreme individualism is the extent to which Sheila represents the effects of broad cultural changes leading to what they, in an introduction to the tenth-anniversary edition to *Habits,* term a "crisis of civic membership" — a crisis that they argue extends even to the heart of the church.[26]

With the spread of such culturally constituted ways of understanding personal experience and justifying decisions, our society lacks the moral coherence of personal character and the institutions — such as churches — that form such character.[27] Yet such character, and the institutions that sustain and are sustained by it, require some places in which identities grounded in the secondary language of biblical faith can be formed for the sake not first of our national society, important as that may be, but of our faithfulness as the body of Christ in the world. As I noted in chapter one, pastoral leaders are just as likely to have been formed by the emotion-driven therapeutic mode and the results-driven managerial mode especially dominant among the educated middle class in the United States. A major stumbling block to receiving God's gift of faith is that we too often make faith a means, a tool to use in achieving effective resolution to organizational problems or to achieve self-enhancement. Faith and even the fundamental commitment to a church becomes a self-maximizing means to life success. For the pastor, faith can be used to bring about organizational success, and for the parishioner, faith offers a possible means to feeling (fill in the blank: peace, wholeness, healing, loved, needed). What has

25. Bellah et al., *Habits,* 221; see also Bruce A. Greer and Wade Clark Roof, "Desperately Seeking Sheila: Locating Religious Privatism in American Society," *Journal for the Scientific Study of Religion* 31 (1992): 346-52.

26. Robert N. Bellah et al., "Individualism and the Crisis of Civic Membership," *Christian Century,* May 8, 1996, 514-15.

27. Robert N. Bellah et al., *The Good Society* (New York: Alfred A. Knopf, 1991); Wuthnow, *Loose Connections: Joining Together in America's Fragmented Communities* (Cambridge: Harvard University Press, 2002).

dropped out is God's active work claiming us as "chosen" and "beloved." Without such vital divine presence that transforms our lives and orients our living towards a good beyond ourselves, we are left with a thin faith aimed at helping us to improve our circumstances or at least feel better about them.[28]

The primary cultural language of individualism is very familiar both to pastoral leaders and to the communities they lead. They already know that slipping into this primary language of individualism — perhaps especially when talking about faith — is often easier than the hard work of consciously speaking in a secondary language of the biblical and theological tradition of Christian faith. They understand what is lost: the pastor as theologian, seeking God's will rather than his or her own, and a community shaped according to normative convictions rather than "what works" or "what I like." Many pastors long to grow in their ability to model and mediate a strong and substantive vision of Christian faith and feel that little matters more than this in their ministry. And indeed, Bellah argues that, while individualism is our "primary language," we have not lost the resources found in our "secondary languages," including what he calls the biblical tradition. Recovering the vibrancy of biblical and theological claims on Christian life can aid us in moderating the impact of self-focused and morally vacuous individualism. In the biblical tradition, the aim is not to self-maximize or self-realize but to respond to God's call to a community in which a genuinely ethical and spiritual life can be lived.

The major obstacles that I've outlined in chapters two and three combine to form a worrisome scenario for pastoral leadership in the church. These twin dynamics — the compartmentalizing and individualizing of our lives — have broadly shaped a trend over decades in which the church thinks of itself as a separate gathering, a sphere of its own. Here pastoral leaders offer effective management and empathetic

---

28. Such a faith funds the sort of "improve your life" message at such megachurches as Lakewood Church in Houston, where Pastor Joel Osteen's motto for the congregation is "Discover the Champion in You!" While the Bible at times draws on sports analogies, as in Hebrews 12, the champion is Christ and the race promises — for us as for Jesus Christ, whom we follow — shame and suffering.

presence within a gathered community cut off from a lively sense of its fundamental theological purpose in gathering: to be forgiven, empowered, and equipped to be scattered out into the world as seeds, as salt, light, or yeast, transforming the world just as we have begun to be transformed by the Spirit of Christ that lives in us. I shall return to this problem in part three of the book, where I sketch a renewed understanding of congregational life that holds together the tension of gathering and scattering, and the pastoral leadership needed to foster and equip such a dynamic life in Christ.

Next, however, I want to turn to a set of specific engagements with spheres of life. These are, as Weber admits, false constructs or ideal types. They do not exist in some sort of hermetic simplicity in the real world. But their reality as distinct and formative in the ways Weber suggests makes it worth the simplification in order for the work of reflective deliberation, theological discernment, and strategic thinking to allow faith to assert its proper role in orienting discipleship in all spheres of life. While I cannot consider all relevant spheres of life, I have considered four. I invite and encourage you to explore others in the way you find modeled in what follows.

PART TWO

Pastoral Leadership and Christian Practice

So, given the social and cultural forces that shape and define us, how can pastoral leaders effectively model and mediate the power of faith to orient discipleship in the various spheres of life — family, work, politics, and the arts? For each sphere I will describe the problems and prospects of living out a faith that matters. As I move through these chapters discussing spheres that we often experience as fragmented pieces of life, I hope to model the practice of thinking theologically. Such thinking is, I believe, crucial to a full understanding of pastoral excellence. By encouraging the practical skill of thinking theologically about everyday matters, this book aims to help pastoral leaders (and those with whom they work in their ministry) find a way to live faithfully in the world.

Each of the chapters in part two follows a similar pattern, dealing with one of the distinct spheres of our society (and of our lives). First I will sketch a vignette to show the tensions between faith and how we often live within these spheres of life. These are personal stories about my own struggle to be a faithful disciple. I think such stories are critical, since pastoral leaders are first of all *disciples* themselves and their work is to foster lively discipleship through their ministries. In order to do the work of fostering discipleship, pastoral leaders must find faith as a way of life compelling and be able to model it in their own life as disciples.

After offering a story, the chapters will circle through a reflective process the Faith as a Way of Life Project used to pursue the question of how to encourage and sustain pastoral excellence. First, I will try to make clear how the social-structural and cultural realities outlined in part one of the book come to bear within that sphere. Second, I will propose some biblical and theological resources that evoke a vision of faith's impact on the realities facing us. In some cases, this means sketching an all-too-inadequate theology to fit the sphere, but in each case I point to other resources that go further. Finally, I'll rehearse an example of pastoral leadership in relation to a Christian practice, modeling the kind of leadership able to hold the vision of a Christian way of living in the world in tension with the real obstacles we face. Through examples of pastoral leadership in Christian practice, enacted in congregations, persons and whole communities can be drawn more deeply into the gathering and scattering of Christ's body for the sake of the world. The final chapter will pull these threads together by suggesting an image of the congregation as "inspired" (from the Latin *inspirare*, to breathe into) by God. The congregation is a living organism, the body of Christ (1 Corinthians 12), whose gathering and scattering, like inhaling and exhaling, is its God-given, life-giving rhythm.

The first sphere I will turn to is first in more than one respect: the sphere of family and friends, or *kinship* as Max Weber called it. The sphere of kinship refers to marriage and children, but also much more: it is fundamentally about social life, about larger circles of family and friends, the circles of trust and affection that extend over years. Yet in a culture of self-maximization, too often our pleasures and taste become the guiding principle even for our most intimate circle of association. In this "foundational" sphere we face our first challenge to make faith matter.

CHAPTER FOUR

Kinship and the Family

A typical morning at our house begins around 5:00 A.M. I roll out of bed and head to the kitchen for a cup of coffee. Then I settle into the oversized blue chair in the sunroom, where, on a good day, I have an hour or so for prayer and quiet work before a thump on the ceiling and the shuffle of little footsteps on the stairs lets me know I'm about to have a sleepy child in my lap looking to snuggle. The next couple of hours are entirely taken up by the work of preparing for the day — packing lunches, getting breakfast on the table and then cleaned up, making sure kids are dressed, teeth brushed, hair combed, shoes found, and homework finished. Oh, yes: my wife Sonja and I need to get ready ourselves! While in one sense the focus is right — we're paying detailed attention to ourselves and especially our children — in another sense it seems that without faith's influence this routine is liable to lead us astray.

With life so wrapped up in such mundane routines and concerns, it is easy for me to fall into the trap of thinking of family as primarily our nuclear family — Sonja, Isaiah, Grace, and me. Too often the assumption among Christians is that the most important meaning of family is exactly this: dad, mom, and children. While it is true that for many people family often does mean some configuration of parents and children, when seen from the perspective of biblical faith, kinship is not such a simple equation. As Christians, we are faced with the startling challenge of Jesus' definition of family as "whoever does the will of God." According to the Gospel of Mark,

A crowd was sitting around Jesus; and they said to him, "Your mother and your brothers and sisters are outside, asking for you." And he replied, "Who are my mother and my brothers?" And looking at those who sat around him, he said, "Here are my mother and my brothers! Whoever does the will of God is my brother and sister and mother." (Mark 3:32-35, NRSV)

Such a "whoever" definition clearly does not begin with a nuclear family model — in fact it sidesteps biology altogether! Rather, such a definition shifts our human biological connections to a secondary position behind our primary bond to the family that seeks to live out God's call.

Littered with Idols

God's call comes to us in the midst of life — life that is God's gift as a work of creation. But because we are selfish, prone to grasp this gift as our own possession, God's call comes to us as a redemptive work bringing us to "new life" in Christ. Such a call comes first of all in the bracing message, "Repent! For the Kingdom of God has come near!" It is a clarion call to face the fact that we are in rebellion from God, working at cross-purposes, fooling ourselves that we can have our own little kingdom shaped by our desires alone. Without the bracing call of Jesus to consider our family as "whoever does the will of God," family can become a false god, a little kingdom we choose and foster by a worship made up of tremendous sacrifices of time and resources.

When family life is arranged by our own desires into such carefully constructed worlds, the power of faith to orient our convictions and actions is thwarted. Danielle, a pastor specializing in work with youth and family in Minneapolis, sees clearly how the teens in her church reflect our consumer-driven culture and speak in the language of our common American individualism, placing private desires before all else. That her teenagers fall prey to these cultural forces says very little about Danielle and a lot about the power of American culture. In fact,

Rev. Danielle Jones

Some time ago I started a weekly gathering of juniors and seniors at a local coffee shop. For an hour and a half we discuss things that are on their hearts and minds — and the topic that we focus on each week is completely student-driven and student-led. My presence as their youth pastor is merely to participate and to ask what I like to call "clarifying" questions — questions that make the students think a little bit more about what they are saying.

As we spent time digging into how we could see God calling us to respond to issues of faithfulness and social justice, interesting comments and conversations came up. I have been amazed at the savvy of many of the students, the ways they understand scripture and their willingness to engage the tough questions of faith and faithfulness. What has shocked me has been the way we close each week.

With about fifteen minutes left we have a common youth group tradition of sharing prayer requests. One by one students go around and ask for prayer for the things that are going on in their lives. Common requests include prayers for success on an upcoming test, help in finalizing spring break plans, and that God would give them the right internship or help them get into the right college. In three months the prayers have not even once focused on the topic that was discussed — but instead always focus on the individual needs of each student.

When I asked about this obvious disconnect, the students responded to me with blank stares. We talk about the things we talk about because they are important, but we talk to God about what we know we need.

she's a wonderful youth pastor who has struggled to help kids and their extended networks of family and friends seek abundant life centered in Jesus Christ. But exactly because she's struggled with this task, she also has a palpable feel for the difficulty in connecting faith to family life.

While Danielle knows it is very important to create this space to listen and encourage conversation about faith, she also finds herself frustrated by the disconnect between broadening conversations over the hour and a half and the contraction back to the self when prayer time comes. Even when discussing social issues that seem to have direct connections to their faith — pressing issues from their lives such as temptations of sex and drugs, relationships with family and friends, and global poverty — their discussions are in a sense one step removed from God. They don't need to talk about God in order to talk about pressure to take drugs or lie to their parents. And when they do bring God into the picture, it is an image of God that Miroslav Volf calls "God the Santa Claus." This God, Volf writes, is the "god of consumerist materialism whose sole purpose is to give." The Santa Claus God "gives without conditions and without demands. As the sun shines and as a spring flows, so God gives — solves our problems, fulfills our desires, and makes us feel good."[1]

In a nationwide study of faith and teens, sociologist Christian Smith has confirmed that this "God as Santa Claus" version of faith is indeed common. In his book *Soul Searching: The Religious and Spiritual Lives of American Teenagers,* Smith writes that

> the *de facto* religious faith of the majority of American teens is "Moralistic Therapeutic Deism." God exists. God created the world. God set up some kind of moral structure. God wants me to be nice. He wants me to be pleasant, wants me to get along with people. That's teen morality. The purpose of life is to be happy and feel good, and good people go to heaven. And nearly everyone's good. This God is not demanding. He actually can't be, since his job is to solve our problems and make people feel good.[2]

1. Miroslav Volf, *Free of Charge: Giving and Forgiving in a Culture Stripped of Grace* (Grand Rapids: Zondervan Press, 2005), 27.

2. Christian Smith, quoted in Michael Cromartie, "What American Teenagers Believe: A Conversation with Christian Smith," *Books & Culture: A Christian Review,* January/February 2005, available at http://www.ctlibrary.com/bc/2005/janfeb/4.10.html (accessed February 25, 2007). See also Christian Smith with Melinda Lundquist Denton,

Danielle's youth group shows an impressive savvy in "the ways they understand scripture and their willingness to engage the tough questions of faith and faithfulness." But they are so captive to individualism that while they are able to share their opinions freely on this or that issue, they can barely see what God might be for if not to listen to their needs and, insofar as possible, fulfill them. Because they are so busy and come from homes where parents are busy, the most important influences that shape them come through their peer culture — music, television, movies, video games, and perhaps most powerfully, advertising.[3]

Young people need to learn a language of faith that can give them alternatives to the "it's all about me" culture — and that's exactly what Danielle is trying to teach them. She knows that in order to become fluent in the language of faith, young people have to be around others who understand faith deeply and can offer the chance to learn and practice it. Yet this doesn't happen very often today, as Christian Smith discovered:

> I don't know how much teens are hearing other people speak the language well, and it really struck us in our research that very few teens are getting a chance to practice talking about their faith. We were dumbfounded by the number of teens who told us we were the first adults who had asked them what they believed. One said: "I do not know. No one has ever asked me that before."[4]

Unfortunately, Smith found that in the structure of teenagers' lives, time for engagement with faith is squeezed. Despite her good inten-

---

Soul Searching: The Religious and Spiritual Lives of American Teenagers (New York: Oxford University Press, 2005), 162-63.

3. Robert J. Coen, Senior Vice President and Forecasting Director at Universal McCann in New York, in his annual June "Insiders Report" on global advertising expenditures predicted total U.S. advertising spending at $286.4 billion for 2006 and $303 billion for 2007 (available in pdf from http://www.universalmccann.com/, accessed February 25, 2007). In comparison, total K-12 U.S. spending on education was $536 billion for 2004-2005 (10 Facts about K-12 Education Funding in pdf form at http://www.ed.gov/about/overview/fed/10facts/index.html, accessed February 25, 2007).

4. In Cromartie, "What American Teenagers Believe."

tions, Danielle's group meets only once a week. And if such conversation has no resonance at home, it is unlikely that this single hour could have a major effect on teenagers' lives.

Kinship networks of love and support can make a powerful difference in the lives of young people. Parents, aunts and uncles, and other adult friends need to be both available in a real and accessible way and solidly grounded in the secondary language of genuine faith. It is striking to hear Danielle say that many of her kids haven't had a substantial conversation with a parent for weeks. One might surmise that many of these teens have learned exactly what their parents have taught them![5] Children learn by example. When those who love them believe in a God who is primarily a source of unconditional love and affirmation, whose main job is to shower blessings of every sort onto those who have faith, Danielle worries — and we should worry too. A view of God that extends only as far as the needs we can think of at any given moment does not point us to the God we meet in Jesus Christ.

Danielle believes that too often we live a life that is "littered with idols" — the material things we desire, worship, and then cast aside when they disappoint us, only to lurch after the next gleam or glitter around the corner. Instead of this manic life in search of the thing that will truly satisfy us, Danielle thinks we need to "fall madly, deeply, and wholly in love with our Savior. It is not to be a life of adequate replacements, but is to be a life of real encounters with the living God." Such an encounter with the living God reframes efforts to successfully engage one's "little kingdom" of the nuclear family. Even more than we need "strong" Christian parents to model "strong" Christian faith, Christians need to embrace the gospel message of family and kinship

---

5. Despite the ways men and women play different sorts of roles, and in many cases log unequal amounts of time in the caregiver role, the cultural layer of seeking self-actualization and fulfillment shapes these different modes of care. Here I'm thinking of Bradford Wilcox, *Soft Patriarchs* (Chicago: University of Chicago Press, 2004) and Don Browning, Bonnie J. Miller-McLemore, Pamela D. Couture, K. Brynolf Lyon, and Robert M. Franklin, *From Culture Wars to Common Ground: Religion and the American Family Debate,* 2nd ed. (Louisville: Westminster/John Knox, 2000).

that calls us out of our family havens, set up according to and for the fulfillment of our own desires, and into the Kingdom of God. When we are so called, family life takes on a much different character.

Whoever!

As my own children grow older year by year, with my oldest nearing the threshold of the teens, I wonder how our family is and could be different than the families Danielle works with. Does the mundane routine of our life *really* challenge the dominant reality so powerfully shaping our sense of kinship and family according to values of desire and pleasure? Does our daily life find its heartbeat in the gift of unsettling grace that comes from new life in Christ?

My worry is, of course, that it doesn't. Too often, we likely do what everyone else shaped by our culture of materialism and individualism does — we shape our little haven with the things and people we like most. How should God respond to this? Perhaps by saying, "Fine. You can go your own way, and we'll just see how you like things on your own, cut off from me." Just here, in the grip of sin, cut off from God, we might be left to spiritually shrivel up, alone with what we've been given.

But God doesn't leave us in our self-imposed "slavery" to sin. Scripture speaks of God adopting us, of Jesus befriending us. Such adoption or befriending means that we no longer live for ourselves, but in and through God's work in Jesus Christ by the power of the Holy Spirit. Writing to the church in Galatia, St. Paul argued:

> When the fullness of time had come, God sent his son, born of a woman, born under the law, in order to redeem those who were under the law, so that we might receive adoption as children. And because you are children, God has sent the Spirit of his Son into our hearts, crying "Abba! Father!" So you are no longer a slave but a child, and if a child then also an heir, through God. (Galatians 4:4-7, NRSV)

This is Paul's description of how we are reconciled as part of God's family, and therefore how God shapes us to live as heirs to a reconciled way of life. As we are redeemed from the status of "slave" to the status of member of the family, so we too are called to extend the reach of the love we know in Christ Jesus.

In John's Gospel, Jesus paints another picture of our new life:

> This is my commandment, that you love one another as I have loved you. No one has greater love than this, to lay down one's life for one's friends. You are my friends if you do what I command you. I do not call you servants any longer, because the servant does not know what the master is doing; but I have called you friends, because I have made known to you everything that I have heard from my Father. You did not choose me but I chose you. And I appointed you to go and bear fruit, fruit that will last. . . . (John 15:12-16, NRSV)

In St. Paul, as in the teachings of Jesus, we find our deeply held cultural belief in "freedom of choice" displaced by divine initiative — we are not the "choosers" but the "chosen." Our new role as "friends" of Jesus does not make us, therefore, intimates in a self-enclosed circle of the like-minded. While Jesus' disciples may have desired ongoing meals in private with him, instead he told them that calling them friends meant that they would go out to make new friends for God by living out a life of self-giving love.

If being adopted or befriended by God means being drawn into living out a way of self-giving love, it will have a distinct impact on how we receive and give as individuals, families, and communities of faith. Martin Luther described a movement from God through us to others as the "flow" of God's gifts, including the gift of our very redemption, but also including all the basic things we need for daily sustenance.[6]

---

6. Martin Luther, "Explanation of the First Commandment," *Large Catechism*, p. 389 in *The Book of Concord: The Confessions of the Evangelical Lutheran Church*, ed. Robert Kolb and Timothy Wengert (Minneapolis: Fortress Press, 2000).

No gifts are intended for us alone, though we can and should use the gifts for our own good. Our aim is both to flourish ourselves and to contribute to the flourishing of others. Interpreting Luther on this point, Miroslav Volf gives the example of a family at Christmas.[7] On the one hand, if a family is to celebrate Christmas well, giving ought to be truly joyful, and receiving full of gratitude. This is not giving to make another feel obliged, nor does it seek glory through magnanimous display; instead, true giving seeks to give something of one's self. Such giving within the family both imitates God's own life as Trinity — the mutual self-giving between the three persons overflows as gift to us and all creation — and likewise imitates the outpouring of love seen in the extension of God's own life through the life of the church as Christ's body.

On the other hand, however, if a family gathers only to give within the intimacy of its network of relations, even if its mutual giving is truly joyful and the receiving truly grateful, it falls short of Christian giving. Such giving only among the closely knit does not allow the continued "flow" beyond itself to those who are friends of God. As we who were once enemies of God were given the gift of reconciliation and friendship, so our giving is broken free of our grasp and again flows out to those in need, those for whom it was especially intended by God. In Jesus' own succinct phrase, "Those who are well have no need of a physician, but those who are sick; I have come to call not the righteous but sinners" (Luke 5:31, NRSV). One might have expected him to only interact with the ultra-religious leaders of his day — and in fact many did expect this of him. Yet God's mercy in Jesus continually broke out of the circle of insiders, opening the flow of God's mercy, healing, and justice to outsiders of all sorts.

This means at least two concrete things for those groupings of people we love and depend upon, whether blood relatives or those "adopted" into our circle of affection, our kin "in the Lord." First, it means within our circles of affection that our connection is recalibrated to allow our love to fit within God's loving design. I love

---

7. These sentences draw upon Miroslav Volf, *Free of Charge*, 72.

my wife and children, but "in the Lord"; it is, in a very particular sense, not I who loves them but Christ who lives in me. In Christ I give them what I have, so that they flourish. Second, it means that our circles of affection need to be broken open so that the gifts of God in Christ flowing to me overflow into the hands of those I know and don't know, who are quite possibly "undeserving" and "undesirable" and yet exactly whom God loves.

How do these two concrete truths about kinship gain traction within my daily routine, changing the balance away from potentially self-centered care for children and family toward reference to the larger claims on our shared kinship as friends of God? As I try to integrate them into my life, I find that our family is less centered on making life pleasing and more being shaped in generosity and gratitude by God's presence. In the midst of our busy mornings, we gather around the breakfast table to sing the old hymn (complete with dance motions our kids will find horrifyingly embarrassing in a few more years, but love to act out now): "Now that the daylight fills the sky/ We lift our hearts to God on high/ That God in all we do or say/ Would keep us full of love today." As we embrace in arms "full of love" at the end of the song, the love we share is no longer simply our delight in one another, but now a delight "in the Lord," love tapped into a larger love, meant to overflow from our circle into the day, wherever we go.

Such a dynamic of self-giving within and beyond our circle of love and affection challenges our cultural predisposition to love only what pleases us. True pleasure, it turns out, comes not from collecting pleasing experiences as if we're filling some trophy case. Rather, true pleasure comes from enjoying what God enjoys: the abundant life that overflows through and beyond those we know to those we don't know. While you doubtless have your own examples, it has been important for our family to sponsor Rose Delesani, a child in Malawi, through Save the Children (www.savethechildren.org). Through giving money to support health and education in her village, writing to and receiving letters from Rose, and including her, Malawi, and all people struggling to survive poverty and hunger in our family prayers and daily conversations, we incorporate a person into our family who breaks open our family to God's work for the sake of the most needy and marginalized. This biblical and theological framing of the sphere of kinship stretches far beyond the vision of many Christians in the United States who emphasize a "focus on the family" — meaning by that especially the nuclear family. Without expanding faith's imagination to make connections to this broader vision of kinship, faith's deepest meanings might not hit home.

Pastoral Leadership and Christian Practice

David Matzko McCarthy, in his lovely book *The Good Life: Genuine Christianity for the Middle Class,* shows over and over again how basic practices of faith work to clear out one's life to receive God's grace. We never earn it; God's grace is free. But for any Christians who desire to open themselves to live in accord with the gift of grace, he argues it is essential for them to reframe their understanding of kinship and home. If the body of Christ — understood here as those who do the will of God — is the first "family" for Christians, then one's home and family are not an independent unit or autonomous domain. Rather, homes and families are places that are interconnected, woven into and interrelated to the life of faith shared in that larger network of kin who follow Jesus. This fact impacts the most basic structure of our lives — even to the point that we come to understand that in the most basic sense even time and space are not our own. Especially not, it turns out, in that place we might think it most true: within the walls of our home and in our most intimate relationships.

Practices are basic human activities, shared among people over time, and patterned by culture. Thus, when Christians engage in practices they do so in response to God's actions and for the sake of the world's needs.[8] Leaders help to invite people into practices, describing

---

8. Craig Dykstra and Dorothy Bass, in a definition of practices that has been important for this project generally and my writing in particular, say this: "By 'Christian practices' we mean things Christian people do together over time to address fundamental

their shape and setting the stage for their enactment, but finally it is the people together as disciples of the Lord who enact the practice. Practices such as eating together or praying are individual actions but they are also pieces of a whole way of life. Practices both interconnect with one another and bear within themselves something of the whole faith of which they are part. Such practices help us to embody the truth that as we follow the way of life set before us by Jesus Christ, we are not our own, but belong to God and to one another. In other words, through doing these things, given by God and carried over time by communities of faith, we orient ourselves to patterns of holy living in daily life. Of course, families could engage in any number of practices, including things I've mentioned above: making music and singing, or doing works of justice and mercy. Even the practice I've chosen to focus on below — sharing a meal — has elements of others, such as hospitality, which shows how interconnected practices are.

Eating Together

Eating together is among the most important things humans do. It is of course a basic animal necessity; we must eat to live. Perhaps because of its basic connection to whether we live or die, the preparation and eating of food has developed as a rich aspect of culture. Whether in ordinary daily meals or elaborate multi-day festivals, meals are always near the heart of family and cultural life. The American dream itself — tied as it is to a vision of family and home — includes an idealistic vision of family gathered around a table for food and conversation. The two religious traditions most influential in American life — Judaism and Christianity — both share a focus on eating together, even if in varied and distinct ways.

Yet like so many aspects of life in America, eating together — whether

---

human needs in response to and in light of God's active presence for the life of the world." See Miroslav Volf and Dorothy Bass, eds., *Practicing Theology: Beliefs and Practices in Christian Life* (Grand Rapids: Eerdmans, 2002), 18.

as families at home or together as communities of faith — easily becomes a closed circle of shared enjoyment among friends. The transition of the majority of Americans to suburban and exurban life, complete with cul-de-sac communities and elective segregation, exacerbates this problem of affinity friendships between the like-minded and similarly-heeled.[9] To some extent, any meal sharing is good, and ought to be celebrated in a culture where eating together is on the decline (despite the continuing high value Americans place on it).[10] The frenetic pace of middle-class life today, running from work to school, to the shopping center and then home, has contributed to the phenomenal rise of fast food in our culture. Even with a growing awareness of the problems that come with being a "fast food nation," the attraction of the quick meal, with its lack of social contact and tendency towards unhealthy foods, does not seem to lessen.[11] When Americans do eat together, it is usually with family and friends, the little circles of private taste we nurture for support and companionship amidst life's vicissitudes.

Eating together is one of life's basic goods. Yet if I were only to commend eating with those I love, I would fall short of the claim of the gospel that breaks open my self-chosen circles to those who are outside not only my circle but perhaps on the margins of many of society's circles. Church families are just as susceptible to this dynamic as nuclear families. Families of all sorts, and the church as a kind of metaphorical "family," often give food or money to those who do not have enough to eat, and such generosity assures that the hungry can eat as well. But giving food to the poor somewhere else, however important,

9. Andres Duany, Elizabeth Plater-Zyberk, and Jeff Speck, *Suburban Nation: The Rise of Sprawl and the Decline of the American Dream* (New York: North Point Press, 2001).

10. Robert Putnam, *Bowling Alone: The Collapse and Revival of American Community* (New York: Simon & Schuster, 2001), shows that families eating dinner together declined by a third, from 50 percent to 34 percent, in the last two decades. Yet a Harris-Interactive 2006 study shows the high value placed on eating together (e.g., 54 percent cook dinner at home five nights a week and 62 percent wish they could eat more meals together than they do currently).

11. Eric Schlosser, *Fast Food Nation: The Dark Side of the All-American Meal* (New York: Harper Perennial, 2002).

courts the twin dangers of making another feel indebted or making oneself puffed up through the showy presentation of gifts. To share in the practice of table fellowship means something else; it means giving of oneself.

Here it is helpful to examine the story of David Wood, the pastor of a Baptist church in a small town in Maine. Their church family had to overcome inertia and doubts about their ability to sustain a communal meal that opened their tables to those in their community who are hungry, lonely, or both. As he tells the story, we see how the persistence in enacting a practice, done well, helped deepen the church's understanding of family within the kingdom of God.

Community Supper, First Baptist, Gardiner, Maine

The vision came alive in late Spring 2003 when Ron Webb said it was time to quit talking and get on with feeding the hungry in their community. He raised the question to Pastor David Wood and the rest of their congregation, asking if they were ready to put their faith into action. David thought they were, and so began to set a plan in motion. He and Ron chose a date, made flyers, and planned a menu. David even painted a sign to put out in front of the church. On their first night, they had tables set, food prepared, and servers ready. Less than ten people showed up. David recalls, "I must confess, I was a bit discouraged. Ron was undeterred. He was in this for the long haul."[12]

By fall, the monthly Sunday evening supper was attracting around thirty guests. Within a year's time, the Sunday dinners — now weekly — were attracting upwards of eighty guests. By David's invitation at the local ministerial association, a number of other churches joined in the effort, sharing in rotation the duties of cooking, serving, eating with guests, and cleaning up. On an average night about two-thirds of

---

12. David Wood, "Signs of the Kingdom in Our Midst," First Baptist Church Newsletter, May 2005, available at http://www.firstbaptistgardiner.org/newsletterarchives .htm (accessed February 25, 2007).

attendees are clients also served by the food bank, but others are simply lonely. Ron describes it thus:

> They're for anybody. Most of the people who come aren't members of any of the churches. You'll see people who really need it. And you'll see people who just don't want to be alone for Sunday dinner. It's a hoot! People come in, eat, and then sit around and talk. It pulls us together. We're becoming a community.[13]

While the suppers are always in First Baptist's basement so that people always know where to go, the work has become a shared task among a core of five congregations in Gardiner.

David says the whole scene reminds him of Scripture passages that liken the Kingdom of God to a great banquet: "It is a joy to see our building illuminated each week by this meal and all who come to the table to be fed and to be received by others in the name of Christ." While giving credit to Ron for making the community supper happen, David points beyond the church members to a greater source for their practice: "We now have this marvelous overflowing gathering every Sunday night that brings the needs of our community and the resources of our churches together in a beautiful celebration of abundance, generosity, and good will. If that's not a sign of the Kingdom of God in our midst, what is?"[14]

Pastoral Leadership and Community Practice

In David's description, the practice of eating together, including the hospitality and friendship around meal and table, points to the coherence of commitment that underlies any particular practice and that ties together the various pieces of our lives. The open welcome to the

---

13. Keith Edwards, "Church Suppers Broaden Their Scale," *Kennebec Journal,* April 25, 2005.

14. Wood, "Signs of the Kingdom in Our Midst."

Lord's Supper on Sunday morning practiced in David's church both points them toward a vision of all creation redeemed and gathered around the heavenly banquet table and sends them out into the world where all tables they share — in homes or in a community program helping the materially and socially poor — are under the authority of that vision.

In such a vision of table fellowship, Christians are never simply hosts, but always, even at our own tables in our homes, guests as well. This is largely because the hospitality, food, and love we share are God's, given to us so that we would not only receive what we need but also pass along what we don't. The inclusive invitation offered to us, bringing us forward to gather around the table on Sunday, is an example for other tables we might set for the world. David caught hold of Ron Webb's persistent faith and shared his commitment to do something with the knowledge that some in their community hungered for food, for companionship, and through these tangible things for the love of God that passes all understanding. Here community becomes family and strangers are welcomed as friends.

Kinship must be broken open so that, while those we most love still have our love, the love we offer is God-shaped.[15] Practices like eating together are God-shaped because of the stories of Jesus that they bear. Participating in such practices together with our family of faith provokes a tension with our everyday realities that pulls us towards that God-shaped life. Such God-shaped practices are done in communities where the stories of Jesus are told, where committed disciples like Ron put their faith into action, and where pastoral leaders such as David show in theological reflection on these practices exactly how the practices are God-shaped. Drawing these theological connections between practices and faith, pastoral leaders open themselves to God's Spirit, who works in us so that we are willing to be broken open for this new way of life for the sake the world.

15. I borrow the phrase "God-shaped practice" from a wise and winsome book by Martha Ellen Stortz, *A World according to God: Practices for Putting Faith at the Center of Your Life* (San Francisco: Jossey-Bass, 2004).

CHAPTER FIVE

Work and the Economy

Wham! The hammer smashed into the wall and shards of tile and cement flew to the floor. It felt good finally to get the project under way. We had a bad leak in our old tile shower, and because of the way it was built, the only way to get at the pipe was to break away the tile wall. The bathroom, just off of our bedroom in our New Haven home, was added on to the house in the late 1940s. We decided that we were unlikely to find replacement tile and wouldn't mind a more up-to-date look, so we chose to redo the bathroom. I'm a pastor and practical theologian by vocation, a trade plied largely with a keyboard and aimed at impacting people. But my avocation has always been construction, a trade with a different sort of impact on a different sort of board, brought home by good aim with a hammer.

During evenings after dinner, with the kids settled into bed, I don my old work clothes, gloves, and safety goggles and head into the bathroom for my second shift. While I've done a whole bathroom remodel without hiring contractors before, this time I'm working with Dave, a builder, John, a plumber, and Paul, an electrician. I'm doing the demolition — down to the studs in the walls and floor — and they will put it all back together with the new materials and fixtures. It will be lovely when it is done, and together with the work I've done on a new back deck and the new guest bedroom upstairs it will add significantly to the value of our home. The housing market in our neighborhood has been steady, and were we to sell, we'd likely recoup the money and time we've invested, and then some.

It is tempting to think only about the economic value of such investment. How much might be saved by my labor versus having the contractor do the whole job? What will be gained in resale value by the completion of this project? What is the housing market doing generally, and how has it fluctuated here in our community? Such calculation, if unchecked, stagnates in self-centered accumulation — we invest in what serves our interest financially and, to a lesser extent, our desires aesthetically. This logic fits home improvement projects, but can just as well apply to our regular job, to housework, or even to relationships.

The first language of our culture, especially in its utilitarian individualist forms, offers no larger framework by which to understand and even critique such efforts at self-improvement. And shorn from a broader Christian framework, we might end up on the wrong side of Jesus' strong words about greed. To make his point as powerfully as possible, Jesus told the crowd this parable:

> The land of a rich man produced abundantly. And he thought to himself, "What should I do, for I have no place to store my crops?" Then he said, "I will do this: I will pull down my barns and build larger ones, and there I will store all my grain and my goods. And I will say to my soul, 'Soul, you have ample goods laid up for many years; relax, eat, drink, be merry.'" But God said to him, "You fool! This very night your life is being demanded of you. And the things you have prepared, whose will they be?" So it is with those who store up treasures for themselves but are not rich toward God. (Luke 12:16b-21, NRSV)

The idea of being "rich toward God" does not allow our efforts at work and economic gain to end with our own enjoyment. The rich man's land produces abundantly. That much, apparently, is the fruit of hard work — either by the rich man or more likely by his hired workers. Presumably, his productivity was gained justly. Jesus does not condemn this; given other things he said about good stewardship, Jesus would likely approve of his good work. Yet just at this point, when the rich man ponders what to do with his abundance, Jesus points out the wrong turn in his thinking. His selfish desire to hoard his own material wealth literally consumes him, and Jesus raises the question of purpose: toward what end do we labor? Tellingly, this parable is given as a response to someone in the crowd who asks Jesus to arbitrate a dispute over dividing the family inheritance. The parable has little to do with how much one has; rather, it casts a vision of how hollow — and how dangerous to soul and society — self-maximization can be when it is free to run its course unchecked.

Buy Every Foot of Land

The field of economics is deeply influenced by the rational actor theory — the idea that we each act rationally and deliberately to maximize our own self-interest.[1] Even the many substantial critiques of this theory don't fundamentally challenge the view of basic human aims presupposed by the rational actor theory.[2] Most of these critiques are focused on the rationality of our actions — showing, for instance, that we very often blunder forward driven by habit or chance more than by explicit calculation. The critiques still assume that we are shaped by a culture of choice and an ethos of self-enhancement, though often unreflectively. But such captivity to the logic of a common culture driven by unchecked market values can't alone explain how faith works in the sphere of the economy, can it? Don't other values rise up and put into perspective the famous profit motive that drives capitalist society?

Mark Gornik, a committed and innovative urban church planter

1. Jon Elster, ed., *Rational Choice* (New York: Oxford, 1986); James S. Coleman, *Foundations of Social Theory* (Cambridge: Harvard University Press, 1990).

2. Donald P. Green and Ian Shapiro, *Pathologies of Rational Choice Theory* (New Haven: Yale University Press, 1994). But for a refreshing and thoughtful critique see Duncan Foley, *Adam's Fallacy: A Guide to Economic Theology* (Cambridge: Harvard University Press, 2006).

Mark Gornik

Harlem's African American community traces its history to the early twentieth century, a result of successive residential relegations in Manhattan. Throughout its history, Harlem's residents faced high rents, overcrowding, economic distress, and physical deterioration. These conditions were not random or self-imposed, but determined by forces outside of Harlem, including the public, real estate, and financial sectors. By the 1990s, Harlem had become a "bargain," and the forces of change once again worked against black residents of the city. Residents and businesses now face a dramatic rise in rents, an influx of wealthy new homeowners, and a branding of community. Speculation and profit, not community oriented development, largely defines real estate activity in Harlem. Capital, once unavailable to Harlem as a communal and historical space, is now available for Harlem as an economic space, but only selectively.

How does faith understand the currents of change in Harlem? Is displacement inevitable? Can the direction be changed? While community voices offer strong dissenting viewpoints, harder to hear are

and theological educator, has struggled with these issues, first in a very poor neighborhood in Baltimore and now in another economically marginal community in New York City. His reflection on the context of his ministry in Harlem puts us in direct contact with the dominant values of this sphere of life — especially the singular drive for profit — and shows us how important it is for people of faith to challenge these gods with the God we know in Jesus Christ. Mark has seen these pressures on Harlem's communal life and residential population firsthand as he has struggled to grow NewSong Community Church. Its membership, almost exclusively drawn from the neighborhood nearby, has made low-income housing a key mission. It uses creative means to develop dilapidated properties into viable mixed-use properties, usually including both community space (a preschool, for example) and af-

public and ecclesial voices of nonconformity. The problem begins when the economic narrative of New York is accepted without criticism. Faithful Christians may lament the course of events, but they rarely question the justification of what takes place or believe alternatives can be generated. Therefore a change of urban narrative is required, or at least resistance to conformation to the story of the city traced to New Amsterdam.

Reported to be among the final words of the real estate speculator John Jacob Astor was the wish that "Could I begin life again, knowing what I now know, and had money to invest, I would buy every foot of land on the island of Manhattan." This finds an interesting juxtaposition with the assertion of Abraham Kuyper that "there is not a square inch in the whole of human existence over which Christ, who is sovereign over all, does not cry: 'This belongs to me!'" Here are two very different ways of seeing Harlem. If faith shapes our living, then it must have something substantial to say about the economic life of the city, about the possibility of decent and affordable housing for all, especially the poor.

fordable housing. The odds are nearly impossible that a single person with a vision could marshal people and resources to compete in a housing market where even a row house that requires gutting and total rehabilitation can fetch more than a million dollars. Yet through persistence and a compelling vision spelled out in his remarkable book, *To Live in Peace: Biblical Faith and the Changing Inner City,* Mark calls for "seeking God's shalom in the city."[3] With characteristic creativity, he leverages partnerships with churches as well as private and public funding sources in order to accomplish his goals.

While New York City may be the extreme case, the drive behind

---

3. Mark Gornik, *To Live in Peace: Biblical Faith and the Changing Inner City* (Grand Rapids: Eerdmans, 2002).

viewing Harlem as a bargain to be bought at the expense of the poor emerges from a deep cultural impulse to value cutting costs and turning a profit. As I described it in chapter three above, utilitarian individualism in relation to work and the economy frames our thinking and acting so that individually and corporately we think our *sole* economic purpose is to manage resources so as to improve our position in the marketplace. While participation in the economy can rightly be seen as good and productive work that puts bread on our tables, it has increasingly become disconnected from any framework that would tie notions of work to concerns about the larger common good.

One symptom of this problem, according to sociologist Robert Bellah, is the heightened use of the term "career," while the older term "calling" with its notions of serving the common good fades from view.[4] The drive inherent in work — and economic life generally — in the United States is not just to profit but also to succeed to the limit of one's capacity, to become a "success." Success usually implies not only material rewards but also a sense of larger meaning and purpose. Yet meaning and purpose are usually sought through another form of individualism — the expressive form — that seeks to find inner happiness through a life filled with pleasures and delights. Giving one's all to work is worth the effort because through it you can, as the U.S. Army once put it, "Be all that you can be," not only in economic terms but in terms of self-expression as well.[5]

A major problem with this cultural impulse is the way it obscures the exact concerns Mark Gornik raises in terms of what one sees with

4. Robert N. Bellah et al., *Habits of the Heart: Individualism and Commitment in American Life* (Berkeley: University of California Press, 1996 [1985]), 119. One obvious marker of the waning of our social understanding of the term is the huge investment by Lilly Endowment in its "Vocations Program" and the resulting spate of publications reviving the topic for reconsideration today. See, for example, Mark R. Schwehn and Dorothy C. Bass, *Leading Lives That Matter: What We Should Do and Who We Should Be* (Grand Rapids: Wm. B. Eerdmans, 2006).

5. Such language taps a cultural ethos spreading far beyond the Army, which is of course why the Army found it a useful slogan. See for example, the following book by possibility preacher and leadership guru John C. Maxwell, *Be All You Can Be: A Challenge to Stretch Your God-Given Potential* (Colorado Springs: Victor Press, 2002).

eyes of faith. Does property speculation in Harlem only serve the material and social well-being of the for-profit developer who makes the deal? Perhaps that will be the case when an upwardly mobile career is the plumb line taking the measure of success. But what if, instead, a notion of vocation takes the place of work as success, offering the knowledge that nearly any work can have dignity and purpose in light of its participation in God's purposes?[6] And what if, as in Mark's eloquent vision, Jesus Christ claims all that we are and do as his own, and asks that we contribute our labor to his great work of shalom, with special regard for those who are poor and vulnerable? The question is to what extent we, with Mark, can enact faith as a way of life with the resources to challenge the dominant values orienting our work and our economic life. It is to those resources that we now turn.

Rich toward God

It is disturbing to think that all my work renovating our house might be the equivalent of "building bigger barns," as Jesus so starkly put it in his parable. In the midst of the work renovating our bathroom, I'm forced to pause and reflect on our motivation. To what extent is my family captive to a cultural language that frames our action and words according to the law of rational actor theories of economics? Are we, that is, simply working to maximize profit on our home, in terms of both equity value now and cash value at the projected future date when we sell the house to the person offering the highest price? What language, from which sources, offers us a means to challenge the hegemony of the value of the bargain that turns a profit? How can we understand the sort of work that could make us "rich toward God"?

We do seek to be honest and play by the rules with regard to our own work and in relationship to the other tradespersons with whom we work. But is not cheating really anything to brag about? It is cer-

---

6. As an example, see the story of Dorothy in C. William Pollard, *The Soul of the Firm* (Grand Rapids: Eerdmans, 2000), 46.

tainly not a model of Christian virtue. Christians are called to do more than merely follow the rules, especially if those rules emerge as a result of systems that do not "seek first the Kingdom of God" (Matthew 6:33). But an even more basic question is, to what extent should Christians embrace efforts to do well in economic terms, even if they know they ought to do good as well? How can we be sure to avoid the danger of simply "building bigger barns" to contain our success and focus on the fact that God creates good work and calls us to labor that we might bring forth food from the earth? It makes sense to reflect here on exactly what Christians mean by work, taking into account several key themes from Scripture and the Christian tradition.

From the perspective of faith, work takes on a particular and definite meaning. Though often strenuous, work is not merely toil. Though often done for pay, work is not merely labor to earn income. A basic theological definition of work ought to begin with the claim that at its base our work is "an activity that serves to satisfy human needs."[7] Such a definition is already pregnant with religious values. It reminds us implicitly that work is good, a gift from God.

How do we know work is a gift from God? God's first action in the world is work! According to the first creation account in Genesis, God worked for six days to make the world, and then rested, declaring all creation good. According to the second creation account, God took Adam into the garden of Eden to till it and keep it, allowing him to eat of every tree but one: the tree of the knowledge of good and evil. All our work, then, ought to participate in God's work of making a world that is good. This account helps us to make sense of the fact of our work; but what ought our work to do?

The purpose of work is twofold. First, it is to obtain the necessities of life. This is the point of the creation story in Genesis 2, where God gives creatures the garden "to till and to keep." In return for our labor, we reap the reward of sustenance for ourselves as well as for those who are dependent upon us. But this is not the end of our purpose in

7. Miroslav Volf, *Work in the Power of the Spirit* (New York: Oxford University Press, 1990).

working. Our work is also intended to respond to the needs of those who are vulnerable. And, as Scripture says over and over, we are to have special concern for the needs of the orphan and the widow — a biblical way of saying those who are vulnerable and marginalized. This is not an add-on to the purpose of our work. As St. Paul puts it in Ephesians, we work also "to have something to share with the needy" (Ephesians 4:28).

In this remarkable passage from Ephesians 4, St. Paul points to three elements of getting the basic things we need to exist. As Paul puts it, "Thieves must give up stealing; rather let them labor and work honestly with their own hands, so as to have something to share with the needy" (4:28). We must not steal, which means that we must not take what is not ours in order to advantage ourselves at the expense of others. The second element is the dominant mode of getting in our contemporary society: we "labor and work honestly with our own hands," giving something to get its rough equivalent in return. But Paul's last element, "having something to share with the needy," means that we give what we don't owe, but rather pass on what God has first given to us.[8] From a Christian perspective, theft is obviously wrong, but honest work for honest pay is also not enough by itself. Faith understands work in a way that presses beyond the quid pro quo mode of work to an understanding of work as gift. We can see the logic of this as we reflect on how God's grace transforms our attitudes towards things, others, and ourselves.

The typical American myth of the self-made person leads us to believe that we have what we have because we've earned it.[9] Our conviction regarding the American Dream goes something like this: If you work hard and play by the rules, you will be rewarded in the end. This is true to an extent, isn't it? It plays to our basic understanding of fairness. Even such crazy events as winning the lottery are considered

8. These modes of getting are drawn from and developed further in Miroslav Volf, *Free of Charge: Giving and Forgiving in a Culture Stripped of Grace* (Grand Rapids: Zondervan, 2005), 56-57.

9. Bellah, in *Habits of the Heart*, 32, holds up the example of Ben Franklin as representative figure of the "self-made man" in American mythology.

67

"fair" because everyone who buys a ticket has an equal chance, and if your number comes up, you deserve the spoils.

So what's missing in this view? Christians believe that God has given us everything, from this moment's breath to the talent and strength to work for a living. Our possessions, then, are really our reaching out and grasping God's gifts to us.

If our possessions are not simply our own, but our possession as a result of God's gifts to us, then we can reasonably ask why God gives gifts to us. But first we should explore *how* God gives to us. In chapter four, I began to explicate the idea — drawing from Martin Luther — that God gives to us through human channels. As we receive, so should we pass on what we have received. In his discussion of the first commandment, that "You are to have no other gods" (Exodus 20:3), Luther argues that God alone is worthy of trust because everything comes from God's "hand" insofar as it comes to us as a result of God's command. All people are our neighbors, Luther writes, and

> have received the command to do us all kinds of good. So we receive our blessings not from them, but from God through them. Creatures are only the hands, channels, and means through which God bestows all blessings. For example, he gives to the mother breasts and milk for her infant or gives grain and all sorts of fruits from the earth for sustenance — things that no creature could produce by itself.[10]

We receive the things we need for daily life from God through our neighbors. As we come to understand this, we can see how our work is really our taking hold of these gifts with gratitude.

When we become grateful receivers of the things we need, we too become channels of reciprocal giving. We are to receive, as Moses counsels in Deuteronomy, with open fingers rather than grasping fists

---

10. Martin Luther, "The Large Catechism," 389, in Robert Kolb and Timothy J. Wengert, eds., *The Book of Concord: The Confessions of the Evangelical Lutheran Church* (Minneapolis: Fortress, 2000).

(15:7-8). Christians live within Christ's own life, or rather Christ indwells in us, so that we are freed from the age-old temptation to grasp. From Adam and Eve taking from the only tree that was off limits, to the onslaught of advertising that constantly tells us we are incomplete without this or that material good, humans have been subject to the insatiable desire to grasp more. In Christ we have enough, and we can trust that enough will come, allowing us to open our fists and become, in Miroslav Volf's lovely term, "more-than-enough" people.[11]

We already have, to recall Jesus' parable above, the things that make us "rich toward God." We have fullness of life and riches in Christ, and are drawn into a way of life that seeks to work in order to give — to be open to God's giving through us in whatever capacity we can offer. As the Jubilee tradition Jesus echoes in his opening sermon in his home synagogue suggests, economic riches are not a sign of God's blessing, but rather a sign of the challenge facing us as we respond to Jesus' call to follow and to live the biblical economics of jubilee (Luke 4; Isaiah 61). "More-than-enough" people do not necessarily have "more than enough" in some objective material sense; they do not necessarily give out of the "extra" column of their personal balance sheet. Rather, the phrase describes a disposition of all Christians, no matter their material well-being, to remember our total dependence on God's giving and to protect against unfair growth of economic inequality.[12]

But what, you may ask, do we do in the face of total disregard for this open-handed vision of economics and this generous, purposeful model of work? It is easy to see how my work — whether my vocation teaching and writing or my avocation doing home repair projects — must serve more than my own needs and ought to evidence special consideration for those who are suffering and on the margins. Let's assume I do show this consideration, in all sorts of small and consistent ways. Still, while I know that the plumbers who work in my bathroom receive more than

11. Volf, *Free of Charge*, 109.

12. Here Ched Myers, "God Speed the Year of Jubilee! The Biblical Vision of Sabbath Economics," *Sojourners*, May-June 1998, 32.

adequate pay for their labor, many others here in the United States and abroad labor long hours for less than is required to live — even those who work full-time at the United States minimum wage.

In light of systemic injustice, as Pastor Mark Gornik suggested earlier in this chapter, people of faith can join their voices together in common witness to their understanding of God's economy where all need not have the same amount, but all have enough. Such a witness can rise as a protest to the suffering of some while others "eat, drink and be merry," their wealth carefully stashed away in ever bigger barns. Jesus himself raised this protest when he assumed the voice of the prophets recalling to Israel its Jubilee teachings that were, as I say above, meant to protect against the sharp inequalities that develop over time between rich and poor.[13] Today faith-based campaigners — such as the ONE Campaign to Make Poverty History — draw on these same teachings to lobby political leaders to act against the huge gap between rich and poor nations.[14] Debt relief, economic empowerment, and advantageous trade opportunities can help to turn unjust circumstances into just and equal opportunities for all to have the dignity of work that sustains us and even lets us flourish.[15] Faith-based voices speaking as one are not only changing unjust laws but at the same time reframing the public imagination — from thinking of a "minimum wage" to striving for a "living wage" — in ways that press the values of faith up against the values of the gods of economy.[16]

Pastoral Leadership and Christian Practice

Thus far, we've highlighted some ways our cultural captivity to forms of individualism predispose us to fall sway to the gods of economy,

13. Myers, "God Speed the Year of Jubilee!"; Sharon Ringe, *Jesus, Liberation and the Biblical Jubilee* (Philadelphia: Fortress Press, 1985).

14. www.one.org.

15. www.data.org.

16. Deborah Figart, *Living Wage Movement: Global Perspectives* (New York: Routledge, 2004).

turning our work into selfish pursuit of material gain — or worse, into taking advantage of others in order to line our own pockets. Whether this takes place in real estate speculation, manual labor, or in the knowledge economy where books are written and published, or anywhere else for that matter, living faith as a way of life can orient us to press back against these false claims. The vision of living "richly toward God" emerges out of Jesus' teachings and a scriptural understanding of how God provides for all by giving to all of us through human channels. This vision reframes our work and participation in the economy by offering us a vision of shalom. As "more-than-enough" people, focused on our abundance in Christ rather than the perception of worldly scarcity, we are free to receive and give as we are able and according to our neighbor's need.

In the final section, I highlight a faith practice that offers all people — and especially those who have the specific call to pastoral leadership — a means to "talk themselves" into living faith at work.[17] In her book *Tell It Like It Is: Reclaiming the Practice of Testimony,* Pastor Lillian Daniel defines testimony as a practice consisting of the "spoken story of how you experience God, offered in the context of community worship."[18] As with the practices in other chapters, this practice is but a piece of a whole way of life. It is not any more or less suited to engagement with the world of work than other practices of faith. Yet in the practice of testimony, pastoral leaders have a chance to speak of God and the everyday world of work — and encourage others to do so — in ways that can transform the imagination of persons and communities to see how faith can and does impact the sphere of the economy. Leadership in relation to this practice would likely look different in many different places, but pointing to this particular example brings to the fore what each can do in relation to the overall aim of making faith matter to our work and to the economic life of our communities, nation, and world.

17. Thomas G. Long, *Testimony: Talking Ourselves into Being Christian* (San Francisco: Jossey-Bass, 2004).

18. Lillian Daniel, *Tell It Like It Is: Reclaiming the Practice of Testimony* (Herndon, Va.: The Alban Institute, 2006), 12.

Testimony

Testimony is most commonly thought of in relation to a court case. Before testifying in court, I would be required to swear an oath to tell the "truth, the whole truth, and nothing but the truth, so help me God." So it follows that when I speak of the practice of testimony I point to circumstances in which people speak truthfully about what they have seen, offering the truth for the sake of some larger common good. In the case of courtroom testimony, the truth-speaking is in the service of a fair trial that does justice to the parties involved. The practice of testimony requires that there are witnesses to testify and others to receive and evaluate their testimony. It is a deeply shared practice — one that is possible only in a community that recognizes that temptations to falsehood are strong, but that yearns nonetheless to know what is true and good.

This practice has ancient roots in the Christian community. Very early on, the disciples testified to their conviction that Jesus was Lord — the long-awaited Messiah who would deliver Israel. It was through testimony that the early followers of Jesus shared their convictions about what God had done in Jesus to those they met in synagogues and city squares. Such testimony to the good news of Jesus Christ has taken on various forms in the history of the church, with preaching as one key focal point. Preaching, however, is a midstream activity that exists between the history of the Church and the contemporary community and its life in the world. It is not, therefore, simply the lone voice of the preacher! If the voice of the preacher is true, it will likely evoke testimony in response by the hearers. This may happen in song, in words, or in living actions of love, mercy, and justice in daily life.

Lillian Daniel, an experienced United Church of Christ minister, takes up this practice through her preaching and has encouraged a vital culture of testimony within the congregation as part of its response to God's work in their lives. Of course, Lillian notes that preaching is not always testimony, for the latter requires an element of personal disclosure. In the example discussed below, Lillian had taken on a three-part sermon series about work during the period when the Faith as a Way of Life Project was considering issues of faith and work. Rather than discuss these issues together at Yale, we traveled to Arkansas to learn about the real-life circumstances of a major Fortune 100 business, Tyson Foods. In one of her sermons, Lillian attempted to describe various work settings at Tyson — settings very different than her own. Through preaching about the biblical and theological meaning of work, and giving testimony to how God works in our lives at work, she makes clear that God claims all these work situations. Therefore all work situations are connected to faith's convictions and directions for living.

Preaching Faith and Work,
First Congregational Church, Glen Ellyn, Illinois

Glen Ellyn, the community where Lillian serves as senior minister of the Congregational church, is a well-heeled Chicago suburban community. Many of her parishioners are professionals of various sorts, including a significant number of managers and other businesspeople. She timed the sermon series during the period our group was considering the relation of faith and work, allowing our work and hers to intersect. Her first sermon addressed biblical and theological understandings of work; the second and third took up paid and volunteer work, respectively. She chose biblical texts that helped to illumine each topic, and each sermon in its own way illuminated a powerful vision of work from God's perspective.[19]

As she began her sermon on paid work, she read the passage from St. Paul in which he argues that for our work to last it must be built on the foundation of Jesus Christ. Much of what we do, Paul suggests, is built on other foundations and driven by other motivations; this work will not be judged worthy and will be burned away by the cleansing

19. For the first sermon, she preached on the parable of the laborers in the vineyard, from Matthew 20; in the last sermon she preached regarding the many gifts among the members of the body, drawing on Romans 12.

fire of Christ's judgment upon his return. Our work, Paul warns, "will be shown for what it is, because the Day will bring it to light" (I Corinthians 3:13). It is an intense text to pick, considering the value and virtue of our daily work and the work of others we connect to as producers and consumers.

Her sermon begins by detailing the complexity of Tyson Foods, a company with a major stake in one of the most difficult industries and struggling to emerge from significant ethics and labor troubles. Yet, Lillian notes, John Tyson, the current chairman and grandson of the company founder, has struck out on a bold initiative to reform the family business, including adopting a statement of core values centered on this: "We strive to honor God and be respectful of each other, our customers, and other stake holders."[20] Lillian also portrays the complexity of our group from Yale with whom she traveled to visit Tyson Foods. This group, she noted, includes a broad spectrum of theological, ideological, and geographical locations, among other differences.

Not surprisingly, Lillian continues, this diverse group came with many preconceived notions and strongly held convictions about what we'd find in our visit. The debates started almost as soon as we convened, but to lift us out of this and give us a bigger perspective, a colleague described his own research on how people integrate faith and work. Using a four-quadrant model he called the "4 E's," David Miller unpacked how people often lead with one sort of means to engage faith at work, when they do so at all. The first, *ethics,* is an obvious candidate, and the second, *evangelism,* is similarly common. The third, *enrichment,* relates to personal devotional practices. The fourth, *experiential,* points to how some people have a deep conviction that their work itself is living faith out in the world — what some might refer to as a "calling."[21] She recounts this background for her congregation partly to prepare them to go with her into the workplace, but also as a

20. http://www.tyson.com/Corporate/CoreValues.aspx (retrieved December 15, 2006).

21. David W. Miller has described this model in his *God at Work: The History and Promise of the Faith at Work Movement* (New York: Oxford University Press, 2007), 126-42.

way to equip them to think about their own life, faith, and work. Up to this point, she has been, according to her definition, preaching without testifying, and as she makes the move into describing the chicken plant she shifts to the "I" language of testimony.

The heart of Lillian's sermon describes her personal journey into the "Chick 'N' Quick" processing plant and, following directly afterwards, a visit to corporate headquarters. She admits having never experienced a factory floor before, and she was amazed by the chill and overwhelming sight of mass raw meat. She notes that many employees were Latina women. She connects this to her later conversations with middle managers, in whose perspective the line worker's jobs are the "first rung on the economic ladder." Lillian was struck by the gaps between rich and poor in this one-day tour from factory floor to corporate boardroom. She asked managers how the core values, especially honoring God, impacted those line workers making $8.60 an hour. As she listened to them talk about the company's commitment to providing workplace chaplains and to offering a "faith-friendly" work environment in which people can talk about their faith, Lillian reflected on how their responses fit within one quadrant of the "4 E's" — enrichment — and her impulse was to raise questions about ethics and about social justice issues related to inequality of salary and benefits.

Her testimony, in fact, presents her own wrestling over complex issues in relationship to a varied set of jobs, all in the context of a scripture passage that asks us to consider what of our work will endure. In the end, she finds power and comfort in the promise of the Hebrew concept *avodah*, a term with layers of meaning including labor, worship, and service:[22]

This is what I find I cling to in the Christian understanding of work — that in our work it's not that the job is bad or good, but if we can bring to it this combination of labor, worship, and service. It's not enough that we see only our own work this way; when we bite into a chicken patty, we should stop and imagine every worker

22. David Miller develops the meanings of the term *avodah* in *God at Work, 6*.

who was part of that and acknowledge the honor, the dignity, the work, the worship, the service in all labor. All of it has value. It is not an accident that our central sacrament takes place around a table. And all of us come to it, nobody getting more or less than others. It's a reminder that all of us bring our work, our dignity, our labor and our service to that one table, and that is where we are ultimately fed. Amen.

Pastoral Leadership

Through this example of testimony in preaching, Lillian tells the truth about some particular real jobs in which people of faith face real difficulties. Through evoking these realities, she makes clear that work is a domain within rather than beyond the reach of faith's influence. She concludes with a powerful affirmation of the goodness of work, its everyday value, and the call to live according to a vision that makes equal space for all rather than accepting radical inequality of position, opportunity, and reward. She finds a way to evoke the very real world of work — calling forth an "amen" by those who put in long hours at their own jobs week in and week out. As part of her sermon, Lillian notes how commonly pastors ignore the world of work and the ways faith connects to what people do Monday through Friday. In working to overcome, then, what many describe as a "Sunday-Monday gap," she takes the next step to evoke God's call to make our selves and our work available to God's vision of a life of dignity for all.[23]

We are challenged to see work not as our ability to leverage our labor for our rewards, but, through claiming God's role as giver of all things, to see even our work as abundant gift. Practices like testimony allow us to enter into Spirit-informed communal reflection about how we are fulfilled as human beings and then to witness to that vision of abundance. The ubiquity of the market and its dominant value in im-

23. John D. Beckett, *Mastering Monday: A Guide to Integrating Faith and Work* (Downers Grove, Ill.: InterVarsity Press, 2006).

proving the bottom line can be challenged by this process of reframing: as people of faith, we ask, What is the bottom line? And it turns out that our bottom line privileges a vision of participation in God's great economy of abundance, working in order to live and to give, living richly in God as "more-than-enough" people. In addition, our efforts to see that vision shape our world force us at times to raise our voice and vote against structures and systems that crush some in abject poverty while allowing others to live in overabundance. It is here that we begin to see one way that the sphere of work and the economy interconnects with the sphere of citizenship and the government. We turn to that sphere next.

CHAPTER SIX

Citizenship and the Government

One night at the dinner table, I noticed my eight-year-old son Isaiah playing with his ear of corn. Before I could say anything, I was stunned into silence by what he was doing. Holding his ear of corn vertically on the plate with one hand, he flew his other hand towards the corn saying, "And here comes the plane flying into the tower." We had not been talking about September 11, 2001. We had not been talking about war or global politics at all that day. We were enjoying a weekend meal on vacation with family in rural New Hampshire. At that moment it became clear to me how profoundly his life is marked by the horror of that day.

In response to September 11, Isaiah made his first effort to connect his faith and the world of politics. We were very worried about exposing him (then only three and a half years old) to too much of the outrage, sadness, and fear we felt in those next days and weeks. Yet we had dear friends in New York, and our anxiety about them coupled with our general reaction filtered through to him loud and clear. He began to call it the "bad bad thing." "Why," he would say, "did those men do that bad, bad thing?" To which we would say, "We don't know, honey, we just don't understand." We prayed for everyone we could think of, including President Bush and Osama Bin Laden. We talked together about the need to pray for leaders, and the difficult challenge Jesus gave us to pray for our enemies.

In the weeks that followed, it became clear that we would attack Afghanistan, seeking to destroy Al Qaeda and punish Afghanistan's Taliban leaders for giving Al Qaeda safe harbor. One morning in October 2001, Isaiah suggested that perhaps he could write to President Bush and send him two paper clips. He reasoned that if the president were to wear one paper clip and Osama Bin Laden were to wear the other, then they would know not to fight. I had chosen as a young man to commit myself to the discipline of Christian peacemaking. As part of that commitment, I took up the practice of wearing a paper clip on my shirt as a witness for peace. The practice grew out of the Norwegian Church's resistance to Germany's occupation during World War II. Bishop Berggrav emboldened a peaceful resistance with his preaching. As part of the resistance, schoolchildren began to wear paper clips as a sign rejecting the power of the Nazis and their racist policies. While the Nazi soldiers would constantly remove the paper clips in irritation, the schoolchildren always seemed to find more.[1] Isaiah had tried to remove the paper clips on my shirts many times, leading to conversation between us about this unusual peacemaking practice.

Isaiah wrote his letter and sent it off to the White House, complete with two paper clips attached to the top of the letter. As a parent, I was moved by his vision and insight. But was I also being naïve? Can I really expect anyone to take this example to heart as a guide to faith's role in the political sphere? Can I seriously take issue with Madeleine Albright, who argued in a speech at Yale Divinity School that it "would be preposterous to apply Jesus' teachings about not resisting evil and turning the other cheek to contemporary challenges in foreign policy"?[2]

On the surface of things, to do so certainly does seem naïve. We did not receive a letter in reply and soon after, President Bush led the United States into an open-ended "war against terror" first in Afghani-

---

1. Inspired by this story from Norway, children in a small Tennessee town attempted to collect 6 million paper clips as a means to understand the enormity of the Holocaust's six million deaths. See Peter and Dagmar Schroeder, *Six Million Paper Clips: The Making of a Children's Holocaust Memorial* (Minneapolis: Kar-Ben Publishing, 2004).

2. Madeleine Albright has since published a book on the theme of her lecture titled *The Mighty and the Almighty: Reflections on America, God, and World Affairs* (New York: HarperCollins, 2006).

stan and then in Iraq. Our city and even our church were soon awash in flags, patriotism, and righteous condemnation of the enemy. As one member of the church council where I was pastor at the time remarked, "It is not our job to judge the terrorists — that's God's job. Our job is to arrange their meeting." To some it seemed that faith convictions were too fragile and unsophisticated to make the transition from our hearts and minds to the halls of power and political realism. To others such convictions didn't belong there in the first place — God who is in heaven lets us work out our own path regarding the gods of the nation. Both groups, however, seem to set human limits on the God-inspired vision of life Jesus called his followers to live:

> Blessed are the poor in spirit, for theirs is the kingdom of heaven. Blessed are those who mourn, for they will be comforted. Blessed are the meek, for they will inherit the earth. Blessed are those who hunger and thirst for righteousness, for they will be filled. Blessed are the merciful, for they will receive mercy. Blessed are the pure in heart, for they will see God. Blessed are the peacemakers, for they will be called children of God. Blessed are those who are persecuted for righteousness' sake, for theirs is the kingdom of heaven. Blessed are you when people revile you and persecute you and utter all kinds of evil against you falsely on my account. Rejoice and be glad, for your reward is great in heaven, for in the same way they persecuted the prophets who were before you. (Matthew 5:3-12, NRSV)

This passage is a clarion call by Jesus to open our lives so that he might live in us — and by doing so, make us children of God. We do not cease to be children of God, even when we tackle the most complicated political issues of our day.

Trapped by Culture's Claims

It is disturbing that when we do meekly insert a vision of a peacemaking God into the political sphere, the gods of nation and war shout us down. It is more disturbing that a vision of a peacemaking God has no privilege of place alongside other visions like, say, one of wanton destruction in the name of attacking "those evil terrorists." Indeed, both the call for peace and the call to war can easily fit within a kind of expressive individualism that seeks primarily to voice its opinion. Such personal expression can feel like a means of discharging political responsibility, while in reality larger institutions such as the government retain the power to shape the course of the nation and the world.

The influence of a therapeutic culture and its infatuation with techniques for health and wholeness impact our thinking more than we recognize. It's not hard to imagine a prescription for good health along these lines: exercise/meditate/do yoga, eat your fresh fruit/fiber/wheat-grass juice, and be sure to express your opinion at least once a day. Average citizens may support or reject national political decisions but generally see them as beyond their control. Whether from despair or disinterest, we retract our sphere of concern to our little slice of life where we can find some modest pleasures and exert some modest control.

New Haven pastor and Christian theologian Joseph Cumming, who lived for fifteen years in a North African Muslim nation, brings an international — and specifically a Muslim — perspective to American life. Why, Joseph wonders, are people of faith in the United States so ready to disconnect faith from the political realm, especially when the gods of war call for the allegiance we owe to God alone? In such difficult situations, faith more typically plays a consoling role in our personal lives than a public role impacting our convictions and actions in the political sphere. Oh, we may write a letter to the president or another political leader, and we may even be the unusual citizen who casts a vote as often as two times in a year, both in the primary and in the general election. As Joseph laments, however, a cultural captivity to expressive modes combined with our sense of the separation of spheres of life seems to severely limit our ability to connect our faith with the sphere of citizenship.

While Joseph doesn't say so explicitly, he clearly implies that Christians have a presumption towards peace and ought to have grave con-

Joseph Cumming

The decision to go to war, or support such an action, is one of the most important moral decisions a Christian can make in the sphere of politics. We might expect that Christian decision-making about war would be shaped by Christian faith. Nonetheless, in March 2003, during the week before the U.S. commenced hostilities in Iraq, only 10 percent of Americans considered their religious beliefs to be the most important influence in shaping their opinions about the war. Among those who regularly attend religious services the percentage was only slightly higher — 17 percent. Only one-third of Americans reported that religious leaders had had at least some influence on their views on the war, and only 11 percent reported that religious leaders had been highly influential. By contrast, 53 percent of Americans said that friends and family had influenced their views on the war, and 43 percent said that political commentators had influenced them.

This failure of Christian decision-making on the war occurred despite the fact that Christian religious leaders of all persuasions had spoken out publicly about the moral implications of the proposed war. Data from a Pew poll suggest that failure to communicate was indeed a problem. Only 21 percent of Americans who regularly attend religious services reported that the clergy at their local place of worship had taken a stand for or against the war. Fourteen percent of lo-

cerns about any war — which by definition suggests that human beings will die and the human and natural environment will suffer terrible damage. As a former Marine, Joseph is not at all naïve about the gods of war and the compelling nature of a call to serve the greater good of the nation. Yet his relationship to Jesus, while not necessarily preventing him from supporting war in very specific and tragic circumstances, figures fundamentally in his judgments about when war is justified.

How can it be, then, that in our most recent plunge into war, in a nation where nine out of ten people consistently report belief in God,

cal clergy took an anti-war position, and 7 percent took a pro-war position, while 75 percent of local clergy either took no position or did not speak about the war at all. These data would suggest not so much that ordinary believers rejected the pleas of their local clergy, but rather that the local clergy did not pass on the pleas of the senior leadership of their religious communities.

This accords with empirical research conducted by Ralph Premdas on the relationship between the church and intercommunal conflicts in a number of countries around the world. Premdas found "that the inter-communal antipathies present in society at large are reflected in the attitudes of churches and their adherents." Though clergy often seek to play a role in reconciliation, "the reconciling thrust quickly evaporates after the initial effort." This is due to the "inter-locking relations of church and cultural section," so that both clergy and ordinary believers are often "trapped within the claims of their own ethnic or cultural community." Is it possible, as Premdas suggested, that the Americans who endorsed the war were so "trapped within the claims of their own ethnic or cultural community" that they were persuaded even to modify their traditional Christian religious beliefs? If Christian faith is to have any credibility in relation to whether and how American Christians think "Christianly" about the major moral and political issues of our day, then it is imperative that we give serious attention to how Christians think about the war in Iraq.

only one in ten people would turn to religious convictions to evaluate the war? How can it be, further, that only one in five of those who regularly attend church would turn to those convictions? Joseph partly faults local pastors for lack of leadership. This assessment is just as disturbing: among the leadership of the church founded by the Prince of Peace, called as they are to be peacemakers, only one in four took any public position, effectively leaving their congregations to flap in the wind of media hype and political posturing.

War is the most extreme manifestation of politics with which the church has to engage. So it makes sense that the general malaise Americans feel towards politics would shape their reactions in time of war as it does in less turbulent periods. When our lives are so caught up in pursuit of career success and the pleasure of family intimacy, the individualism driving our vision of life fits best with personal and local expressions of community. Local volunteerism offers a feeling of "giving back" to the community — a kind of citizenship offering — in return for what is mainly a self-absorbed life. Churches both provide an affirmation of God's love for each individual and a social network for community volunteerism.[3] Both personal affirmation and social networks are highly sought after by the large and highly mobile middle class in America. Yet, as Robert Bellah explains, Americans often have great difficulty connecting this local and personal sense of community involvement "to the large-scale forces and institutions shaping our lives."[4]

The disconnect between individual pursuits of goods and the larger forces governing society betrays a worrisome abandonment of the sphere of politics to the rules of power and national interest. Absent clear leadership, such structural forces and political realities are difficult to understand. In response to this complexity, our default mode is retreat — to family, church, and the everydayness of work — leaving the world's mess to the professional politicians and government officials. While Americans still value local civic involvement (which they do not usually consider "politics") and are drawn to symbolic shows of national political support (especially in times of war), they strangely disparage that important middle ground where most political decisions are made: the competing interests reflected in electoral politics.[5] What Joseph discovered and laments is the way our primary language of indi-

---

3. Robert Wuthnow, "Reassembling the Civic Church: The Changing Role of Congregations in American Civil Society," in Richard Madsen, William M. Sullivan, Ann Swidler, and Steven M. Tipton, *Meaning and Modernity: Religion, Polity, and Self* (Berkeley: University of California Press, 2002), 163-80.

4. Robert N. Bellah et al., *Habits of the Heart: Individualism and Commitment in American Life* (Berkeley: University of California Press, 1996 [1985]), 199.

5. Bellah, *Habits of the Heart*, 200-201.

vidualism predisposes us to individual faith disconnected from the larger system of electoral politics, leaving us with underdeveloped skills for thinking about how, in times of war or peace, to relate the fundamentals of our faith to the fundamental processes of our democratic republic. While Christians are certainly not alone in facing the problem of the disconnect between the personal and the political, Christian faith properly understood should draw us into political commitment.

Blessed Are the Peacemakers

Earlier, I said that "on the surface" actions like Isaiah's letter to President Bush seem not to have any effect. Yet faith-based advocacy on issues as diverse as poverty, abortion, or school choice has indeed had powerful, if varied, impacts. On the surface, we know that such individual expression of opinion (called "deliverables" by activists who try to develop these special purpose groups) can make a powerful difference when coordinated into a coherent campaign.[6] But how do such letter-writing campaigns escape being simply another vehicle for a culture of individualism to seek self-expression and, if possible, exert power to achieve self-serving aims? More to the point, what would distinguish our household's modest political action in the name of peacemaking from such self-serving actions so typical of groups from the NRA to the AARP?

If we look a little deeper, might there be more to such a naïve offering of faith than I've allowed thus far? To answer affirmatively, as I want to, I have to first consider what God might want from politics. Second, I can ask how such actions on the part of Christians — whether in their role as citizens in general or even as elected officials — might cooperate with God's purposes for government. Asking and answering these two questions can help us to see how to more faithfully connect our Christian convictions to the sphere of politics.

6. Robert Wuthnow, *Restructuring of American Religion: Society and Faith Since World War II* (Princeton: Princeton University Press, 1990), 100-132.

First, let's consider what Christians have understood to be God's purpose for government. We need not resolve the longstanding debate among Christians regarding the origins of government in order to say what God might want from politics. Regardless of whether politics were created by God as part of creation for the good work of ordering human society or whether social governance was created after sin entered the world as a means to contain evil and protect the innocent, we clearly now see that politics is a process shot through with compromised people, ideals, and actions. St. Paul understood the government to do God's will insofar as it keeps order, protects the innocent, and punishes the evildoer (Romans 13). While the modern nation-state has much more complex functions, we might theologically describe its core tasks simply: as God's (perhaps unknowing) servant, it orders social life for the good of all, both helping the weak and hampering those who do wrong.

A Christian understanding of the power of government always understands it as subservient to God. While perhaps the noblest ideal offered by the nation is the honor of dying at war in her defense, even such a sacrifice cannot be understood simply as the highest good for a Christian. The call to serve the nation is, properly speaking, always to be judged in light of God's ultimate calling upon our lives. Drawing on the words of St. Peter — "We must obey God rather than any human authority" (Acts 5:29, NRSV) — Christians have defended acts of civil disobedience and the right to judge wars to be unjust and immoral.

Martin Luther, no pacifist to be sure, still argued strenuously that Christian citizens — especially those in an office of political leadership — order their action first in relation to God. Commenting on Jesus' teaching quoted above, "Blessed are the peacemakers, for they shall be called the children of God," Luther argues,

> Therefore anyone who claims to be a Christian and a child of God, not only does not start war or unrest; but he also gives help and counsel on the side of peace wherever he can, even though there may have been a just and adequate cause for going to war. It is sad

enough if one has tried everything and nothing helps, and then he has to defend himself, to protect his land and people.[7]

As he so often does, here Luther gives both a negative injunction — do not start war or unrest — and offers encouragement to do whatever one can to assure peace. With sorrow, Luther admits to the possibility of necessary war, but only for the sake of self-defense and through the legitimate channel of the government.

Luther does not give government authorities free rein. He strongly cautions even those in office to honor Jesus' call to be peacemakers to the limit of their ability. He argues that Jesus

> gives the name "peacemakers," in the first place, to those who help make peace among lands and people, like pious princes, counselors, or jurists, to people in government who hold their rule and reign for the sake of peace; and in the second place, to pious citizens and neighbors who with their salutary and good tongues adjust, reconcile, and settle quarrels and tensions.[8]

Luther's division between leaders and ordinary citizens translates differently into our setting in a modern democratic republic where each citizen has a role to play in political life through voting in elections, binding us to our representatives in ways the peasant and the prince in the late middle ages never imagined.

Those who are in leadership as teachers and preachers of faith, according to Luther, have a special responsibility to speak of faith's claims to those with political responsibility. "Whoever has been commissioned with this office, must administer it. And it is wrong for him to neglect it or to be so scared that he refuses to open his mouth and to denounce what should be denounced, irrespective of personal considerations."[9] Yet, as he argues above, one must only do so for the sake of

7. Martin Luther, "The Sermon on the Mount," in *Luther's Works*, vol. 21, ed. and trans. Jaroslav Pelikan (Saint Louis: Concordia Publishing House, 1956), 40.

8. Luther, "Sermon on the Mount," 41.

9. Luther, "Sermon on the Mount," 120.

others; for himself, he says, "I am perfectly willing to let them have whatever temporal goods, power, and prestige God gives them; and I would do my best to help them keep it all."[10] Here Luther outlines a twofold approach: doing all one can to seek justice and peace for the neighbor, while giving up calculations that would figure in personal gain.

With Luther we see the subtlety of the different modes for working towards the peacemaking we are called to in Christ. Some of these modes, such as seeking justice without personal gain, every person — Christian or not — can pursue. However, the love of enemies is a work Christ specifically commanded of Christians; his offensive impartiality echoes God's own. As Luther says, imagining God's perspective: "'For whom do I bear my beautiful fruits and berries? For the vilest rogues and rascals on earth.'"[11] And as God does, so should we.

But how, in political life, where power and personal interest preside, does one do as God does? And how does one differentiate acting from self-interest and doing God's will? To return to my example of Isaiah's letter writing, how might such politically engaged actions on the part of Christians — whether in their role as citizens in general or even as elected officials — cooperate with God's purposes for government? Here it makes sense to recall our discussion of how God gives in the previous chapter. There I described how God gives through channels. We not only receive but also pass on the gifts, becoming the channels — the means — through which God cares for all.

It may be helpful to consider how our channeling of God's gifts fits into the context of politics — specifically as it relates to an attack upon our nation. How do we respond to our enemies in faithful political action? Miroslav Volf, echoing in part what Martin Luther argued before him, suggests a difference between how we respond as individuals and the response of the state. Because, while we were enemies of God, we were made one with God through God's self-sacrifice in Christ Jesus for our sake, we should embody such love towards our enemies.

10. Luther, "Sermon on the Mount," 120.
11. Luther, "Sermon on the Mount," 126.

Because God forgives all, we too can forgive any act of violence or harm, including the terrible acts of September 11. It is important to say that the act of forgiveness does not absolve wrongdoers of their wrong; rather, forgiveness is to accuse, and yet to forego punishment. The gift of forgiveness contains the assertion of injustice done, and to accept the offer of forgiveness, the wrongdoer must accept the charge of guilt alongside the offer of release from guilt. But since God in Christ died for all, we can make an offer of forgiveness based on the knowledge that we are already forgiven by God. Whether or not the wrongdoer receives that gift — from God or from me — is another question altogether. That is because acceptance of guilt is the necessary precursor to its removal, and its removal is the gift, not the offer in itself.

The state, on the other hand, as well as a Christian acting in an official capacity for the state, ought to seek the protection of the vulnerable and restrain the wrongdoer. "Discipline for the sake of a wrongdoer's reform and the protection of the pubic is compatible with forgiveness," according to Volf. He continues, however, echoing Martin Luther's comments about restraint. While discipline and protection are called for, "retribution is not. Those who forgive will have a system of discipline, but retribution will not be part of it. They ought to forgive rather than punish because God in Christ forgave. Christ is the end of retribution."[12] One can imagine elected officials following disciplinary processes through multilateral channels in response to a belligerent ruler rather than embarking on a campaign of preemptive war.

One might now have the capacity to see how, as a citizen, Isaiah's letter with paper clips attached was not simply his effort to express his — or my — view, as any individual shaped by our culture of emotion and emoting would expect. Nor were he and I simply joining a political bloc trying to shape public policy to our taste. Rather, living rooted in God's forgiveness, we live in Christ as channels of God's gifts for the sake of the world. Our desire to serve our own interests is overcome by

---

12. Miroslav Volf, *Free of Charge: Giving and Forgiving in a Culture Stripped of Grace* (Grand Rapids: Zondervan, 2005), 170.

seeking God's will and cooperating with God's work. Bold as this may be to say, we can act and trust that God's will be done through us. Speaking out on behalf of peace and forgiveness is faith in action joined to a coherent, communal, Christian witness for the common good God has in mind for all creation.

Such action, to recall Robert Bellah's terms from chapter three, depends on an important secondary language in American culture — the biblical tradition. Yet in order for this tradition's language to overcome our primary language of individualism, we need to learn its full range; we need to practice connecting faith to all spheres of life, including politics. Too often, as Joseph Cumming points out in his reflections, Christians — even pastors — don't practice making these connections. The enormous number of pages written on America's so-called "separation" of church and state has no doubt influenced the perception of many Christians and their pastors regarding the importance of keeping the church out of politics.[13]

While the so-called Religious Right did attempt to make significant political inroads during the 1990s, this movement is starting to backfire. Various evangelical voices are loudly decrying the de facto marriage of churches and a particular political agenda, and rightly so.[14] Should this mean Christians are uninvolved in politics? Should pastors cease to speak to their members who work in government, especially if they are in elected office, about the role of faith and political leadership? Scripture and the teachings of our best theological traditions would quickly say No. Jesus calls us to blessed living "on earth, as it is in heaven," to a vocation vigorously pursued in public life for the sake of the good of all.

13. Among the best new treatments of this difficult question is Noah Feldman, *Divided by God: America's Church-State Problem — and What We Should Do about It* (New York: Farrar, Straus, and Giroux, 2006).

14. Jim Wallis, *God's Politics: Why the Right Gets It Wrong and the Left Doesn't Get It, a New Vision for Faith and Politics in America* (New York: HarperSanFrancisco, 2005); Randall Balmer, *Thy Kingdom Come: An Evangelical's Lament, How the Religious Right Distorts the Faith and Threatens America* (New York: Basic Books, 2006), and perhaps most interesting, the work of an evangelical megachurch pastor, Gregory Boyd, *The Myth of a Christian Nation: How the Quest for Political Power Is Destroying the Church* (Grand Rapids: Zondervan, 2005).

Pastoral Leadership and Christian Practice

In this chapter I've focused on the danger of reducing political participation to an expressive outburst of individual views. The intertwining
of individualism and the value of power-driven self-interest in the
sphere of politics too often causes people of faith to stumble when they
try to engage faithfully in public life. Yet Christ's call to be peacemakers, to discern ways to speak and act responsibly both as citizens and
government officials, challenges us to find means to overcome these
obstacles to faithful living. Thinking through how faith can lead us to
action that protects the innocent and builds up the common good is
hard work that comes through practice in community. As those called
to be peacemakers for the sake of the Prince of Peace, we must avoid
the temptation to leave the sphere of politics to its own values, or in
what amounts to the same thing in the end, to offer proposals so naïve
as to be practically irrelevant.

In these last pages, I again highlight an example of a faith practice
— communal discernment — and a pastor who encourages this practice through her work. While many practices, including communal
song or praying and acting for justice (as in the Civil Rights movement
of the 1960s), might have powerful roles to play in helping us connect
faith and politics, the practice of discernment seems particularly apt. It
offers a measure of calm reflection grounded in seeking God's will,
which in our current climate of shrill and combative politics seems
nothing less than inspired. To such a divisive time in our polity, the
Christian community can and should offer something more than hard-
edged rhetoric that adds to the fire. We might add a healing balm to
our body politic, bringing hope for a deeper and more truly human
politics that draws closer to the purposes of God.

Practicing Communal Discernment

Communal discernment requires the hard work of thinking together
with the community of faith, deliberating about significant issues, and

seeking holy wisdom regarding why one proposal versus another offers the best way forward. Christians believe that we are not "independent selves" but belong to Christ, and to his body the Church, and are called to live lives of receiving and passing on God's gifts. So it is a mistake to imagine that we think and act on our own, according to our personal opinion, in the public life of our nation and world. Discernment in community as a means to understanding God's will is an essential practice as Christians seek to be faithful citizens.

"Hot off the Press,"
First Presbyterian Church, Concord, California

Pastor Mary Naegeli, senior pastor of a downtown Presbyterian church near San Francisco, cannot abide our current disconnect between politics and the life of faith. Her congregation does not know her political party preference, a fact she takes great pride in, but she leaves no room for confusion over her feelings about the importance of faith for living as citizens. Her adult education class, "Hot off the Press," might be called a school for faith-based citizens to learn how to draw on their faith in their roles as citizens in city, nation, and world.

Mary is pastor of First Presbyterian Church in Concord, California, a thirty-minute drive from San Francisco. Mary ministers to a diverse crowd including typical suburban families and longtime Concord residents, faith seekers and lifelong Presbyterians. Her driving goal as a pastor is to learn how to ask the right questions to help people grow in faith and to align themselves with the life of Christ. One key way she has done this is through a long-term coaching effort that takes place during "Hot off the Press." Mary explains the class:

> The idea is to engage in discussion of world and national events from a faith perspective. My agenda has been to model and teach "ordinary" Christians how to think Christianly, in a world that often values feelings more than rationality. Each week I bring a news story that begs for a Christian response. We read it together and

brainstorm on the issues it raises. We then consider what God might say about the situation and what actions we might take in response.

The Sunday I visited, the news article was about the street protests over treatment of immigrants in France. The article, from a local newspaper, presented multiple voices, including leaders in the immigrant communities and various French politicians and government officials. We first needed to sort out as best we could what facts could be known. Mary pushed hard to separate out opinion and bias such as "The French have a sense of nationalism rooted in racial purity" and discern the actual shape of the circumstance. The interaction of the twenty-five or so participants was lively and responsive to her prodding. They clearly knew the drill, policing each other as much as Mary did regarding the effort to sketch a factual basis for the discussion. Then Mary introduced several Scripture passages, including passages from Deuteronomy on treatment of the "alien" and Galatians 3:28 regarding oneness in Christ. Mary's clarity about Scripture's importance for considering the issue did not collapse into any direct policy recommendations; rather, it gave way to a vigorous conversation about the complexity of law, immigration, and issues California faces that are similar to the French case.

Pastoral Leadership

Practicing thinking about faith in relation to immigration in France teaches that faith matters in all spheres of life. Such guided conversation (Mary laughingly calls herself a "referee") trains Christians how to see and act with eyes and legs of faith rather than be guided by the many other orienting forces in their lives. The sessions are both real and rehearsal. In one sense, because of their use of the day's newspaper, the sessions are real. The members together parse issues that face their church, town, nation, and world that day, finding ways to connect their faith to how they think about or get involved with these issues. Whether members of the group currently work in government or are ordinary citizens, the exercise directly informs the kinds of judgments and actions they might make. At the same time, these sessions also serve as rehearsals of how one might discern Christian approaches with a group on any issue.

Overwhelming issues, from healthcare to the muddy debates over war and peace, face us as we think and act as citizens. Our national tradition of church and state separation coupled with a culture of individualism predisposes us to be too easily satisfied with personal expression as a form of politics, whether that takes the form of privately griping or mailing our check to the group or leader of our choice. Leaders in the church are easily swept along with these currents, especially when they are busy planning worship and caring for the personal pastoral needs of their flock. Yet the practice of communal discernment teaches us — as a starting place — how to let faith shape our lives in the sphere of citizenship and political life. If God is Lord of heaven and earth, not just the Church, then we might know that God is already at work in the sphere of government. We are called, here as everywhere, to channel God's gifts.

CHAPTER SEVEN

Leisure and the Arts

As we headed across midtown Manhattan packed in our taxi, I tried to imagine what Dizzy's Club would be like. Broadway. Jazz at Lincoln Center. The Time Warner Building. This was the big time in the Big Apple, and I could hardly wait. As we hopped out of our taxi and paid the driver a handsome amount for the few blocks we'd traveled from our hotel, I looked at the busy street, the lights shining through the large glass doors and the huge atrium beyond. We were swept in, following people up the elevators to a velvet-roped line outside the fifth-floor room. Posters of jazz luminaries and the hushed tones of those already in line gave the atmosphere a sort of reverence. With a group of colleagues from the Faith as a Way of Life Project, I was going to hear a saxophone player named Joe Lovano. While he seemed to be a big name, I didn't know his work. It didn't matter — that he was playing this show at Dizzy's Club was enough for me.

Before long, to raucous applause, Lovano walked out with his elderly piano accompanist. I didn't know this pianist's name, but he seemed frail and nearly fell as he ascended the steps to the stage. Upon recovery, he smiled and waved gingerly before taking his seat. While this beginning worried me, as he began to play his age melted away and the magic of his nimble fingers took over.

We watched over the next hour as our imagined luminary, Joe Lovano, sought ways to step back and highlight this stoop-shouldered pianist whose subtle tones and energetic playing had captured the

95

room. The real luminary turned out to be the one unknown to me: we later found out that this venerable man was Hank Jones, a true jazz legend still playing at the age of eighty-nine. During one particularly stunning moment, Joe Lovano simply stopped playing and walked to the back of the stage, giving over the music to this joyful and soulful man. As the song wound to its end, a man two tables to the right of us shot up, shouting and clapping as if his life depended on the tribute he was offering.

I should have known that something deep and moving might happen. Caught up in the excitement, I simply let myself expect good music at an exciting venue in exchange for my ticket price. This was no church experience, and so what business did I have expecting a transcendent moment? Yet the sphere of arts and culture is the realm of imagination, the realm where one can commonly hear terms such as "spirited" or "soulful" and where fans show "religious" devotion to their favorites. People whose art is extraordinary are often described as "inspired." This should point those of us who believe that everything beautiful comes from God to the notion that the Spirit of our Lord breathes through a saxophone just as much as through the sighs of pious prayers. What I saw as Joe Lovano stepped back to let Hank Jones soar pointed to nothing less than the very power and glory of God made flesh. Incarnational moments are not simply or strictly defined by the historical life of Jesus or by his presence in the Eucharistic elements on this or that congregation's altar table.

In the poetic prologue to John's Gospel, an Incarnational vision of life — including the arts — carries echoes of God's original creation of the world.

In the beginning was the Word, and the Word was with God, and the Word was God. He was in the beginning with God. All things came into being through him, and without him not one thing came into being. . . . And the Word became flesh and lived among us, and we have seen his glory, the glory as of a father's only son, full of grace and truth. (John 1:1-3, 14, NRSV)

All things, the text says, came into being through him. Not one thing — not Joe Lovano's saxophone, nor Hank Jones's piano, nor even Dizzy's Club full of jazz lovers on that late October evening — came into being without him. In this sense, as Luther memorably put it, "Christ fills all creation like wheat fills a sack."[1] This is a powerful vision, a bifocal vision, seeing what things appear to be and what they are in their fullness as they come from and belong to God.

Choose between the Two

How does such dual vision — seeing material things and their relation to God — shape our approach to integrating faith with the sphere of arts and culture? Can this call to incarnational living as participants in God's abundant life help bring both visions of the world together into a coherent form of life? When we simply pursue our own "thing" — whatever that may be — in the arts, we risk following the whims of our desires separated from the vision of the God-shaped meaning of the arts found in Christian community. When this solo pursuit is driven by inner whim or current tastes within some mode of cultural expression, we can find a solely self-serving pursuit of success, pleasure, or recognition. Tension between pursuit of success by solely artistic standards and submission to the larger purposes of God has shaped the life and work of Mako Fujimura. A talented artist and deacon of his Presbyterian church in New York City, Mako sees how the "arts scene" demands that young artists deny the influences from their communities and faith traditions in order to offer their full devotion to the "splendor of the medium." They succumb to the temptation to withdraw into a little world of expression and taste. They buy the warped view of individual success that so easily leads to grandstanding and arrogance typical in the highly competitive world of the arts. On the

---

1. Martin Luther, "The Sacrament of the Body and Blood of Christ — against the Fanatics," trans. Frederick C. Ahrens, in *Luther's Works, American Edition*, vol. 36 (Philadelphia: Fortress Press, 1959), 343.

Makoto Fujimura

For over ten years now, I have been part of a small but fervent community of creative people in Greenwich Village called the Village Church. My life cannot be adequately described, nor my career as an artist explained, apart from this group of believers.

As the Village Church grew, so did my young career as an artist. My two calls — as a church leader and as a painter — had a symbiotic relationship. I found myself juggling the two in sometimes delightful, sometimes chaotic ways. The church took on a life of its own as young creative folks began to flood in. Many had grown up in Christian homes and attended Christian colleges, and had opted to move to New York to pursue their callings as artists, dancers, writers, or performers. Implicit in the New York of the early nineties was the idea that you couldn't have both faith and art at the same time. You had to choose between the two, or at least be satisfied with a sort of a détente. You might survive as a creative Christian, but you were not expected to thrive.

Paying attention to the relationship between creative work and faith became an integral part of my contribution to the church. I began to dream that ours would be a community where people could find their creative voices. What seemed at first like a double calling — to painting and to my church — I began to see as a single call. This call convinced my wife and me to move with our three children to downtown Manhattan, to what is now Ground Zero. It was this call that helped us and our faith community to endure 9/11 — and to decide to stay and take part in the restoration afterward. My family is now marked by history of God's making, both visible and invisible.

other hand, Mako's vision of repentant and humble acceptance of the gift of community feeds his creative fire and grounds him in relationships that remind him who and whose he is.

Art and faith, Mako suggests, find keeping company difficult. The tensions between these worlds are deep and difficult to resolve. Some of these tensions result from the modern separation of style from substance, from the emergence of taste as the criterion for style.[2] In the not-too-distant past, the "high-culture" art world where Mako works would have been the only art world, with a narrow range of noble patrons and portraiture and sacred art its few possible subjects. But with the broadening of the middle class and the rise of mass urbanization on the back of the industrial economy, micro-worlds of taste and cultural production multiplied, creating new forms of art distinct both from the tastes of the upper class and from sacred strictures. Today, both consumers and producers of art face the challenge of allowing their faith to make substantive claims on a variety of forms of art and culture, from film and theatre to pop music, from professional sports to yoga.

When they write about these various forms of art and culture, what may broadly be considered "leisure activities," Robert Bellah and his co-authors draw on the concept of "lifestyle enclaves." The term helps to define both what is distinctive about this amorphous sphere of social life and how it might produce the tensions with faith expressed by Mako above. While the authors of *Habits of the Heart* define community as broad and inclusive of difference, a "lifestyle enclave" is "fundamentally segmental and celebrates the narcissism of similarity."[3] They mean two things by "segmental," both of which are important for my use here. First, a lifestyle enclave (say, jazz lovers or connoisseurs of abstract expressionism) involves only a "segment" of an individual. Usually it is not related to work; it is a pursuit carried out in one's "leisure" time. This meaning connects with Max Weber's description of society's development into various spheres that parallel the compartmentalization of our individual lives. Second, a lifestyle enclave is a social space shared only by those with common interests. Those with common interests fill their time and attention with their

2. See chapter two, as well as Pierre Bourdieu, *Distinction: A Social Critique of the Judgment of Taste* (Cambridge: Harvard University Press, 1984).

3. Robert N. Bellah et al., *Habits of the Heart: Individualism and Commitment in American Life* (Berkeley: University of California Press, 1996 [1985]), 72.

desired pursuits, interacting with others who share those interests, oblivious to those outside their enclave.

As a result of the development of such distinct and self-contained lifestyle enclaves, each driven by values internal to their worlds and grounded in little more than the ebb and flow of popular taste, young people entering the art world are too often drawn into a self-referential lifestyle enclave that asks them to give themselves over to the narrowly construed values internal to the enclave or leave their dreams of a career as an artist aside. At best, Mako suggests, they might compartmentalize, pursuing art according to its own rules and keeping faith in a tidy sphere quite separate from the other. Mako has the support of his faith community, so that while his integration of faith with his art has come at some cost to his success in the art world, he has had the strength of conviction to endure. Despite the fact that he cannot resolve the tensions, he has not given up struggling to make his faith and art into one life. For him, this struggle has been possible because he has been intentional about building a network that will support his work and encourage this melding of faith and the arts. Building on Mako's story, we can consider the resources of faith needed to overcome the divide between faith and the arts and culture, and to lead communities in which such integration can be practiced with vigor.

Two as One

I can laugh now looking back on how even as the leader of a group of pastors coming together to consider faith's connection to the arts, I still went to Dizzy's Club expecting bang for my buck, not to be moved in my soul. I am so much a part of this culture and have been so shaped by the expressive modes of individualism that I quite easily slipped out of thinking Christianly and instead approached the club as just another lifestyle enclave. Here I could feed my personal taste for jazz and add this famous club to the list of jazz venues I'd attended. Why is this bad? The effect of this segmenting of interests into my taste versus yours, fed by the relentless offer of specialty products to suit my particular taste, leads to the creation of a self-centered world, a world untouched by the core purpose of faith.

If we press just a bit further into John's Gospel, the clarity of purpose behind the incarnation, the gift of God's Word made flesh, we find something better than seeking endlessly to satisfy our own desires. Here, adding to the verses from chapter one of John's Gospel quoted above, the whole story is given in brief form:

> He was in the world, and the world came into being through him; yet the world did not know him. He came to what was his own, and his own people did not accept him. But to all who received him, who believed in his name, he gave the power to become children of God, who were born, not of blood or of the will of the flesh or of the will of man, but of God. (John 1:10-14, NRSV)

The Christian faith calls us to become children of God. Christians, according to John, are those who receive Christ, and who believe in his name. This One, who is both wholly God and wholly human, who is in the world and yet not of it, through whom the whole world came into being, this One comes so that we might be born anew "by water and the Spirit" (John 3:5). Afterwards, as Martin Luther writes, "We are Christs — with and without the apostrophe."[4]

God became human for the sake of overcoming our self-centered efforts to find our salvation through worldly pursuits, calling us to repentance and new life through baptism, and into new life in Christ. Therefore, we cannot be truly satisfied by merely joining lifestyle enclaves. We're freed to actually engage broadly in the lives of others, and of our world generally, seeking in Christ to give ourselves away in service to God's purpose of love, mercy, and reconciliation.

The overwhelming grace and mercy present in the text of John's

---

4. "*Christi sumus in nominativo et genitive.*" See Martin Luther, "Sermons on the Gospel of St. John, Chapters 1–4," trans. Martin H. Bertram, in *Luther's Works, American Edition,* vol. 22 (St. Louis: Concordia, 1957), 286.

Gospel prologue means, then, that in Christ, as children of God, we are free, having found the deepest source of satisfaction and meaning to our lives. Luther speaks of the transition from seeking one's own worth to finding one's worth given by grace as the central transition of Christian faith. Making the point that we are freed from a life that seeks its own salvation through particular styles or tastes, Luther states that "once you have become a new person, the new man stops discriminating among types of clothing or kinds of food and drink." The key point here is the source of our salvation, our fullness of worth. If our true value is confirmed in the rebirth we experience by water and the spirit, we are free to find ways to have our lives serve as extensions of God's mercy, love, and justice to others.

How, you might ask, does such theology of incarnation and salvation directly connect to this chapter's discussion of arts and culture? First, I want to examine and critique a very common and problematic view among evangelical Christians today, one with a long history in the Church. The view I refer to draws a bold dividing line between the sinful world and the holy church, between saved persons and those who are lost.[5]

There is certainly valid biblical truth in this view, but it also contains misleading understandings of sin and grace. The view of sin such a position depends upon suggests that sin manifests itself in sinful acts, acts that a Christian does not commit because of the gift of grace. In order to seek a context in which one can live this new life of holiness, such Christians eschew the world and create their own subculture with versions of "worldly" activities now baptized by explicit Christian values. One can easily see the whole world of contemporary Christian music as such a reaction: the baptized can still embrace the sound of electric guitars, but with wholesome lyrics that teach of Christ and his benefits. This view totters on the edge of making the claim, "You are saved by grace, now go and prove it." With this view comes the ever-

---

5. In the following paragraphs, I have learned from Theodore A. Turnau III, "Reflecting Theologically on Popular Culture as Meaningful: The Role of Sin, Grace, and General Revelation," *Calvin Theological Journal* 37 (2002): 270-96.

present danger of "backsliding" into the life of sin and the sinful acts that accompany it.

Please don't misunderstand me: sin understood as acting badly and grace as the power to act rightly is not wholly wrong. The problem is that in this view, too much depends on our ability, and too little on the power of evil and of God. On the one hand, if sins are merely acts, we don't take proper notice of the basic fault of human life that the Reformers in the sixteenth century called *incurvatus in se,* or the self curved in on itself.[6] Misunderstanding the deeply sinful nature of our human existence then allows an overly optimistic sense of how easily such a fault can be overcome simply by trying to hide from bad things. On the other hand, if grace merely gives Christians the power to act rightly, then it limits grace to both a sort of shallow "motivation for doing good" and to a help for Christians alone. If grace is really only for Christians, and only for helping them do good, then we have nearly lost the vision of God's love for the "whole cosmos," as John 3 says in the original Greek, and the nature of an incarnational Word through which all things came to be.

Grace, then, might better be understood as a work of God prior to our salvation, as the capacity for anything to be at all, and as the sense of beauty and possibility that infuses things. Out of this unfathomable grace and love, God seeks to turn us out of self-centeredness and to selflessness, as God is in God's own life as Trinity. Such abundant giving beyond oneself for the sake of a beautiful but broken world where God is already present, already loving and preserving, does not mean retreat from culture. Rather, it means immersion in it for the sake of God's desire to call all creation to new life, to a final reconciliation and peace that the biblical writers called "shalom." If I had had this view in mind as I listened that October night to Joe Lovano and Hank Jones, I might have seen immediately the presence of God's grace flowing into their lives and the moment — irreplaceable and beautiful — in which we shared the transcendence of their music.

---

6. Matt Jenson, *The Gravity of Sin: Augustine, Luther and Barth on 'homo incurvatus in se'* (New York: T&T Clark, 2007).

The idea is not that we simply baptize popular culture as filled with God; some of it is truly awful. Rather, we should simply trust that God's grace is broad enough to be working in the world, in and through arts and culture, and our ability to see the depth present there should allow us to sit and listen fully, deeply, with a generous spirit. C. S. Lewis put it this way: "The first demand any work of any art makes upon us is surrender. Look. Listen. Receive. Get yourself out of the way. (There is no good asking first whether the work before you deserves such a surrender, for until you have surrendered you cannot possibly find out.)"[7] Here, one sees the condensation that the incarnation embodies turned towards the task of engaging all forms of art. By giving ourselves away to the moment, trusting that God's grace both upholds us and has given the world its great beauty, we can make connections between faith and the expressions of producers of culture.

Those connections we discover between, say, the experience of the peace of Christ and the lovely peace evoked by Hank Jones' soulful rendition of "L'Amour de Moy," do not lead to easy slogans or messages about God, Christ, or faith. The connections are not so much that explicit sort, which we're all too familiar and bored with anyhow through the preachy explicitness of products from "Christian" art and culture. Rowan Williams, in conversation with *His Dark Materials* author Philip Pullman, put it this way:

> What you learn, I think, after absorbing a really serious piece of fiction, is not a message. Your world has been expanded, your world has enlarged at the end of it, and the more a writer focuses on a message, the less expansion there'll be. I think that's why sometimes the most successful "Christian" fiction is written by people who are not trying hard to be Christian about it. A bit of paradox, but I'm thinking of Flannery O'Connor, the American writer, my favorite example here. She's somebody who, quite deliberately, doesn't set out to make the points that you might expect

7. C. S. Lewis, *An Experiment in Criticism* (New York: Oxford University Press, 1961), 19.

her to be making, but wants to build a world in which certain things may become plausible, or tangible, but not to get a message across.[8]

Here we find the way to build bridges between the world of faith and the world of the arts. Such a perspective, offered here through Lewis and Williams, provides a means to find the whole, deep, complex, and human reality present in culture, and to seek its meaning in relation to what we understand God to be doing in the world through us. Finding the connections between faith, art, and culture comes not from narrowing, but from expanding and deepening, our engagement with worlds beyond our own. To paraphrase Flannery O'Connor, the arts and cultural expression generally are "about everything human and we are made out of dust, and if you scorn getting yourself dusty, then you shouldn't try" to engage and understand it.[9]

Pastoral Leadership and Christian Practice

This chapter has pointed to the ways we can allow individual taste and personal desire to box us into narrow corners of our own making. Whether someone makes her livelihood in the sphere of art and culture broadly construed, or simply seeks to find solace there through leisure pursuits, the temptation to simply seek common cause with the like-minded tempts us all. Even Christians, it turns out, are subject to forming "lifestyle enclaves" where those who think they've "found it" share in mutual self-delight. God's incarnate word — Jesus Christ — is the love through which all things were made and to which we are all called in repentance and faith. Jesus breaks open the sealed enclosures of desire and expression that lead us astray from what God is doing in the world. Culture — and the imagination that gives rise to the arts of

8. Lyn Haill, ed., *Darkness Illuminated: Platform Discussions on 'His Dark Materials' at the National Theatre* (London: Oberon, 2004), 92-93.

9. Flannery O'Conner, "How to Be a Novelist," in *Mystery and Manners* (New York: Farrar, Straus, and Giroux, 1969), 68.

all sorts — can offer a vision of God's grace in creation and a hope for the kind of abundant life we can share once reconciled to God through the gift of forgiveness and mercy offered for all in Christ. While glimpses of such graced imagination are available to all people, once we are caught by the movement of the Spirit of Christ we are freed from obsession with finding that thing that finally will satisfy our deepest longings. Living in Christ, Christians are freed to join in with the great creative work of God in remaking the whole world into a new and promised shalom.

Making Music as Spiritual Practice

The elemental practice of making music offers an example of how any-one, pastoral leader or street performer, can find deep connections be-tween culture and the One through whom all things were made. Music and ritual have been present at the heart of cultures throughout his-tory. The expressiveness of the human voice, the rhythm in the beating of the human heart and breath, are so elemental that it is easy to see how the practice of music-making connects with all the practices in previous chapters — from the music that might accompany eating to-gether to the ways testimony might be told through song.

Music is deeply human; it vibrates in our very bones, and tells the stories of our lives and cultures.[10] What we sing, or the music we hum, says something profound about who we are and the world in which we live. Music is a way into culture, a basic way we share with others what moves us, express our lives, and find meaning in the day-to-day routines we follow. Music is capable of portraying the full stretch of living — from our deepest sorrows to our most profound joys. While this is true for any people or culture, this is particularly true for com-munities of faith. In Christianity, as in Judaism from which it devel-

10. I draw in these paragraphs from the wonderful book by Don and Emily Saliers, *A Song to Sing, a Life to Live: Reflections on Music as Spiritual Practice* (San Francisco: Jossey-Bass, 2006).

oped, communal song based on the millennia-old texts collected in the Book of Psalms has been central to worship and self-understanding.

Not only is music basic to human life and faith communities; it is basic to personal identity. Singing and listening to songs help us remember significant people and moments. Any time I hear the old Western standard "Red River Valley," I'm taken immediately back to the wilds of Montana where I grew up, and to the memory of my grandfather who so loved that song. Or, in another way, when I hear the powerful civil rights song "We Shall Overcome," my mind flashes to Atlanta, to Auburn Avenue, and to the legacy of Dr. King I experienced so powerfully there. These and many more examples show both how music intertwines with memory and how music is not simply individual but ties us to community, history, and the broader cultures in which we live.

Jazz in the City, Hyde Park Union Church, Chicago

Rev. Susan Johnson's church, Hyde Park Union Church, sits on the University of Chicago campus on the South Side of Chicago. Over her more than twenty years in ministry there, she has found jazz to be an increasingly powerful means to connect faith to the life of the city. The church is surely deeply influenced by the academic culture of its surroundings, but its wider neighborhood also includes the South Side — for the last fifty years or more a predominately African American area of the city that struggles with poverty, urban blight, and crime. Yet this same community has tapped the music culture arising from New Orleans and the Mississippi Delta, and has been a center for jazz and blues music since early in the twentieth century. Among the members of Susan's parish during her many years as pastor, Willie Pickens stands out for his combination of high-level musicianship and deep Christian conviction. Over time Willie's combination of interests led to conversations about bringing these worlds together.

It began simply enough, with Willie playing a specially arranged carol in jazz form during the annual Christmas Eve service. After a few years Susan convinced Willie to do a full-scale jazz Christmas concert with his trio and other guest performers. Over the decade from 1995 to the present, this concert not only drew big-time jazz talent and many fans to consider the moods and melodies of the season of Christ's birth, it also brought the faithful out of their "insider" way of thinking into another mode, expanding their sensibility of what sacred music could and should be. These concerts played a third purpose as well: raising hundreds of thousands of dollars for South Side agencies that care for families and children.

By 2004 the series had gained enough prominence to expand into a series of free sacred jazz concerts for the city. These four concerts featured original arrangements by Willie Pickens, centered on themes of "Theophany," "Unfathomable Love," "Forgiveness," and "Service." Presented through 2004 and 2005, they reached thousands of church folk and jazz folk who saw a moving testimony to the integration of a life in faith and music.

Pastoral Leadership

In fostering a connection between Christian faith and making music, Susan has also fostered connections between the church and the arts community as well as the city as a whole. She, like Mako Fujimura, takes her own commitment to live faith as a way of life and seeks to build bridges that model faith's connections to culture and cultures' deep-rootedness in the fullness of God's creative love.

Reflecting on this ministry, Susan writes that "Jazz in the City is not a ministry I would have anticipated fifteen years ago, which is when the first seeds were sown, but it has had transformative power in our congregation and across the city." Transformative how, I asked her? She responded by talking about how her church's offer of hospitality to the jazz community — and in Chicago, that means hospitality to the African American community as well — has transformed their church, opening them to beauty, to a more inclusive reach, and to one way to show the relation of the Spirit to the spirit of jazz. This sentiment is captured in Lloyd Sachs's review of a concert for the *Chicago Sun-Times:* "The evening's most stirring musical storytelling found Africa Brass transferring the deep, timeless mysteries of the Mississippi River, as captured in Thompson's bold, swelling arrangement of 'Old Man River,' to Biblical streams."[11]

As Susan considers this profound experience in her pastoral leadership at Hyde Park, these themes stand out:

> Honoring the cultural legacy of African Americans without watering it down. And the integrity of both their art and their spirituality and how there is barely enough room for that in Christian worship and piety. In the black church both gospel music and spirituals were not allowed in church at various points in their history. How much more does an interracial church with predominantly white leadership have to learn about what is appropriate and how flexible one can be.

Her humility comes through, as does her determination to foster Christian practice that opens itself to be used by God for the enfolding of art into worship and for reaching out to the city.

11. Lloyd Sachs, "Malachi Thompson & Africa Brass at the Hyde Park Union Church," *Chicago Sun-Times* (May 30, 2000), available at http://www.findarticles.com/p/articles/mi_qn4155/is_20000530/ai_n13864573 (accessed February 27, 2007).

PART THREE

Leading the Gathering and Scattering

In Acts 8, following on the heels of the harrowing story of Stephen's martyrdom, the persecution of the church begins. Driven by his fervor, Saul pressed forward to destroy the church and the text says, "all except the apostles were scattered throughout Judea and Samaria" (Acts 8:1). Such an expectation might be more disconcerting to the reader had Jesus not said this would be so. At the end of Luke's account of the days following Jesus' resurrection, two believers walk to Emmaus with him and he reveals himself through breaking open the Scriptures and a loaf of bread. The next morning, the two returned to Jerusalem, found the community "gathered together," and told them what had happened. While they were gathered, Jesus appeared in their midst. There he rehearsed the reasons for his suffering, death, and resurrection. He promised that the Father would give them what they needed to carry on his work, preaching repentance and forgiveness of sins to all nations. And as the Acts of the Apostles continues Luke's story, Jesus says, "you will receive power when the Holy Spirit comes on you; and you will be my witnesses in Jerusalem, and in all Judea and Samaria, and to the ends of the earth" (Acts 1:8).

Here at the beginnings of the church we see the core impulse that has defined her life ever since. Gathered, we receive God's own self through holy word and holy food; scattered, we carry on Christ's work as his very body, upheld by his very Spirit, proclaiming his truth. This same pattern is at the heart of Jesus' teaching ministry. As an example, take his well-known parable about the farmer sowing seeds. Luke reports that a large crowd gathered together and Jesus told them a parable about the work of scattering. The good news of the Kingdom of God is the seed, and the task is to scatter it so God might work in the lives of those who receive it (Luke 8:4-15). While for the moment Jesus wanted his disciples to keep the good news of this kingdom quiet, their ultimate task was likened to scattering seeds, or in another parable, to shining a lamp in the darkness. Of course, Jesus notes, a lamp shouldn't be hidden under a bed but rather put upon a stand so many can see the light (Luke 8:16). Seeds and light, salt and yeast all do similar work in Jesus' parables of the kingdom — all point to the purpose of Jesus' work and our own. Who we are and are becoming in Christ is all for the sake of the world. We are gathered into Christ's body, the Church, for the work of scattering.

Were the world as it should be, there would be no necessity to scatter into the world. Were there already, as Isaiah (65:17) describes and John's Revelation (21:1) imagines, "a new heaven and a new earth," we could all gather in the presence of God's glory, joining in the heavenly banquet that knows no end. Then there will be no tears, no sorrow, no suffering. Then we will not be scattered out into the darkness to share light. Yet we are now still in the long Saturday, the stretch of time between God's decisive "NO" to the sin and evil of the world through the resurrection of Jesus and that day when God will make all things new. In this "now but not yet" time we ourselves are both now and not yet, and our calling is to embody this pattern of gathering and scattering, worship and mission, celebrating the light of Christ and sharing the light that shines in each of us by the indwelling of his Spirit.

In this final section I consider the shape of pastoral leadership and congregational life that is ready to overcome the obstacles to living faith as a way of life today. The image of gathering and scattering helps us to understand a kind of pastoral leadership that can hold together both an inspiring vision of faith and the worrisome current realities that produce social and cultural obstacles to living the faith daily. The rest of the book, then, might rightly be considered exercises in practical mastery, or in how to regain the creative tension demanded by excellent pastoral leadership.[1]

1. As such, this book has learned from and is a contribution to the current revival of practical theology that arises from and seeks to strengthen the faithful life of disciples for the sake of the world. See Dorothy Bass and Craig Dykstra, eds., *For Life Abundant* (Grand Rapids: Eerdmans, 2008).

CHAPTER EIGHT

Pastoral Leadership for Faith as a Way of Life

Rubber Band Leadership:
Vision, Reality, and Working the Tension

In his work on learning personal mastery, Peter Senge tells the story of Antonio Stradivari and his quest for the best sound that could be produced by a violin.[1] Stradivari spent his entire life in the pursuit of that sound. He made constant refinements to the violins he crafted. Still today, 300 years later, the violins built by Stradivari are considered among the very best available. Senge uses Stradivari as a means to unfold his understanding of practical mastery, and the core process required to achieve it: the process of continual improvement he calls "generative learning." Generative learning emerges when one enters intentionally into the "creative tension" between the current realities, whatever they may be, and the vision of where one wants to be.[2]

Creativity results when one is so unsatisfied with the current situation that one is driven to change it. This drive to change, however, requires that one have a clear understanding of the current reality as well as a specific vision of what ought to be in its place. With an accurate view of reality, one will see the constraints that inhibit the vision; with

1. Peter M. Senge, "Self-Mastery" (videotape, 7 minutes). Chart House International, 221 River Ridge Circle, Burnsville, MN 55337. 1-800-811-5218.

2. These concepts are detailed in Senge's important book *The Fifth Discipline: The Art and Practice of the Learning Organization* (New York: Currency, 1990).

a compelling vision, one can press forward creatively to find ways of working within the constraints in order to achieve the vision.

With some caveats, of course, this model of creative tension can illuminate the church's life in the "long Saturday" between the realities of the world as it is and the promise of a "new thing" already accomplished in Jesus Christ, awaiting its fulfillment.[3] It is too simple to say, however, that somehow the church embodies the vision and the world embodies the reality in need of change. In a very real sense both church and world have within them elements of God's vision of life as it should be and realities of life as it is under conditions of sin, suffering, and human failings. However, in discipleship as well as pastoral leadership, God's promises are uniquely available in the church through a holy presence many churches believe is found in the proclamation of the word and the administration of the sacraments. It is into this presence that the Spirit gathers us, and it is filled with this presence that we are again scattered into the world to work the "creative tension" between the God-filled vision we know to be true and the sinful realities we find in daily life.

Pastoral leadership, at its best, operates in this creative tension between God's gift of abundant life given to us free of charge and vagaries of our human selfishness. But if pastoral leaders lose hold of either the truth of their actual circumstances or God's gift of another way, they also lose the tension, and pastoral leadership bends every which way in response to a variety of impulses.

Slack, Two Ways

It is very difficult to maintain the tension between the new life proclaimed in the gospel and the actual circumstances in which we live and lead. I argue that two main forces cause the tension to slacken: the

3. The finest theological reflection on the Christian life as a "long Saturday" is Alan E. Lewis, *Between Cross and Resurrection: A Theology of Holy Saturday* (Grand Rapids: Eerdmans, 2001).

social differentiation of spheres of life that make our lives feel so fragmented and the culture of individualism that misleads us into thinking
that we can find meaning and purpose in a self-maximizing model for
success. These obstacles to living and leading faith as a way of life
translate into two main problems, problems I pointed to at the ends of
chapters two and three in a direct way and underscored through examples in chapters four through seven. I want to revisit them before suggesting how, on the basis of where we've traveled thus far in the book,
we can find a vision for leadership that tightens up the slack.

First, when the church becomes simply one sphere among various
spheres, offering its relevance in terms of something people need in order to be complete, the tension slackens between the version of life offered in the gospel and the oft-troubled realities of our lives. Too many
people — Christians or not — imagine church and its Sunday morning
worship as offering a respite, a moment of peace and reflection in the
otherwise frenzied week. They imagine it as a place to draw energy, or
imagine it as a "haven in a heartless world."[4] Such an understanding
of church has largely given in to the compartmentalization of life: worship and the church are used in the service of the other spheres of life,
especially work and the economy. When church is viewed this way,
people such as Liz, my parishioner described early in the book, use
Sunday as a well from which to draw energy or peace for the hard
work of making ends meet in the rest of the week. The pastor in this
model of church becomes the manager of the "spiritual sphere," an expert who both assures adequate exposure to things religious for the
membership of the organization and provides spiritual services to the
membership herself.

The second way slack develops between God's intention for our
lives and the realities of our everyday failings comes from the cultural
dominance of America's primary language — individualism. Here, in a
way that intertwines with the structural separation of the church as a

4. The phrase comes from Christopher Lasch, *Haven in a Heartless World: The Family Besieged* (New York: W. W. Norton & Co., 1995). Obviously, Lasch here attaches the
phrase to family. While Lasch argues for the merits of such a view of the family, his conclusions are dubious for the family and impossible to accept for the church.

separate sphere, churches and their worship services become "lifestyle enclaves" where like-minded groups can gather for succor and solace, commonsense advice on marriage, or an inspiring talk that lifts the spirit. In an effort to be accessible and not offend the ideas of genuine seekers, the church enables what amounts to little churches of one all worshipping in their own ways, to their own gods, yet sharing common seating and sanctuaries. The pastor in this model of church becomes the therapist who is always available and yet has nothing to offer but a loving God and personal reassurance that seeks in every case to provide what is desired by the parishioners, as if their demand for spiritual products simply mirrored their demand for life-enhancing products in any other sphere of their lives.

Tightening Up the Slack

Admittedly the two portraits of slacker churches and pastoral leadership within them are unfair caricatures. I've drawn them in a cartoonish sort of way so that, while the truth they bear might strike home with you, they don't really exist as I've described them. These are types of dysfunction all churches in our society struggle with — and we all need to take a hard look at our churches and pastoral leaders with fresh eyes. Insofar as these dysfunctions hold sway, they make faith impotent and the church only faithful to half its mission — which is to say, not faithful at all.

In sharing examples of creative pastoral leadership I have portrayed ways of reeling in the slack, thereby recovering a mode of pastoral leadership that fosters faith's guiding impact on daily living. I've given examples of four congregations and the Christian practices their pastoral leaders have fostered. These pastoral leaders are each recovering pastoral excellence as we've defined it here: shaping communities for living faith as a way of life. What is distinctive about their work when compared to traditional modes of pastoral leadership? I want to try to answer this question as a means to answer the larger question of how to most effectively tighten the slack between God's call to abundant life and the social and cultural obstacles that prevent us from answering with our whole lives.

Some literature on pastoral leadership has used the classical "Threefold Office of Christ," that is, the understanding of Jesus' ministry as inhabiting the offices of Prophet, Priest, and King, as a means to speak of pastoral leadership. In one recent description, Rev. Kate Harvey argues that each of the three offices gives shape to the tasks of ministry leadership.[5] *Prophets* take seriously that communities don't know the way forward and need, on the basis of God's faithfulness and promises, a vision that gives them hope. *Priests* stand in the gap between the sorrows and joys of today and the fullness of God's future. They bear the pain of the world before God while declaring to the world the promised salvation offered in Jesus Christ. *Kings* are those who, in more inclusive parlance, galvanize the church to live within a vision of God's reign realized. These three "offices" of Christ give shape to the ministry in and to the body of Christ, the Church.

Others who are writing about ministry have called upon a more modern triptych: *office, profession,* and *calling.* Gregory Jones and Kevin Armstrong use these three as part of a tri-fold vision of the pastoral vocation.[6] *Calling* points to the integrity, spiritual depth, and maturity of those called to the work of ordained ministry. It carries a sense of divine intervention, seen in some cases as a direct voice speaking to the one called, and in others as a mediated call that comes through community. *Profession* calls to mind the distinction of graduate education and the specialized knowledge imparted for the sake of skilled practice of ministry. But its deeper roots recall religious orders and the "profession" that one makes upon joining a monastic community. *Office* — as explicated above — describes the ways those serving in ordained ministry represent Christ both in the gathered community and to the world.

While these various ways of speaking can bear enormous fruit in ex-

5. Kate Harvey, "Calling Up the Called," in *Sustaining Pastoral Excellence Newsletter* (September 2006), at http://www.divinity.duke.edu/programs/spe/newsletter/200609.html (accessed January 9, 2007).

6. L. Gregory Jones and Kevin R. Armstrong, *Resurrecting Excellence: Shaping Faithful Christian Ministry* (Grand Rapids: Eerdmans, 2006), 80-87.

plicating the shape of pastoral leadership, my usage of the term "pastoral leader" points to a shortcoming in such classic and contemporary modes of describing pastoral work. Not all pastoral leaders play traditional roles of the "pastor" or "priest" — they do not all lead congregations or practice the ministries of preaching, baptizing, and presiding at the Lord's Table. Some pastoral leaders, for example, serve in Catholic settings as lay ecclesial ministers, whereas many churches have lay deacons or youth ministers. Yet each of these leaders is called to lead in ministry, serve to build up the church, and foster discipleship for living faith as a way of life alongside and in much the same manner as those with more traditional roles as pastors, priests, or ministers.

Instead of drawing on classic paradigms, then, I wish to draw out of the examples in chapters four through seven a particular trait I take to be both ancient and necessary for contemporary communities of faith. It is not a model traditionally associated with the *persons* of the ordained clergy but with the *process* of their leadership. The role, developed within the initiation process of the early church, is that of "sponsor" or "spiritual guide." While the role of spiritual guide for those new to the faith was very important in the early church's process of Christian initiation, its role contracted as the church moved into the long Constantinian era, when infant baptism became the norm and parents were the *de facto* spiritual guides for children as they grew in faith. However, as more robust rites of Christian initiation have been recovered over the last few decades in the face of a largely post-Christian North Atlantic world, so has the necessity of a revived model of the spiritual guide.

The sponsor or spiritual guide might sound similar to contemporary talk of pastors as "coaches."[7] The model of "coach" evokes the idea of one-on-one mentoring and encouragement about specific aspects of an overall performance for the sake of a larger goal: winning the game. While I like aspects of the "coach" model, especially its focus on teaching performance, its main reference — to a game — does not

---

7. Among recent titles, see Liz Creswell, *Christ-Centered Coaching: Seven Benefits for Ministry Leaders* (St. Louis: Chalice Press, 2006); Tony Stoltzfus, *Leadership Coaching: The Disciplines, Skills, and Heart of a Christian Coach* (Charleston: BookSurge Press, 2005).

have the same historical and biblical resonance as does a way or journey. It is true that the Apostle Paul used language of "running the race" as an analogy for the Christian life (Hebrews 12:1-2). However, such references are few, and overusing them today may play into the idea that faith, like sports, is an aspect of life one can "take up" and "work on" as a weekend pursuit. Faith, however, is not an add-on in the search for a full life; it is life itself. From God's call to Abram in Genesis and the Exodus and wilderness journey of the Israelites to the call of Jesus to "follow me," the foundational stories of faith speak of our pilgrimage of faith in this life.

While the disciples turned from their former lives and followed Jesus, we are called to believe, to be incorporated into the body of Christ through baptism, and to learn to "walk in newness of life" (Romans 6:4) as part of this community. The very earliest stories we have of conversion show that guidance for those new to faith was offered by sponsors, spiritual guides whose double-edged job was to witness to the community regarding the fitness of the candidate while guiding the candidate in the way of life practiced by the community. Theodore, an early church father, wrote that in preparing for baptism the candidate needed to be released from "citizenship in an earthly and political city [to] citizenship in the heavenly city and kingdom." From the time of enrollment for baptism, sponsors served as spiritual guides to this way of life in the heavenly city:

A duly appointed person inscribes your name in the Church book together with that of your godfather who answers for you and becomes your guide to the city. . . . This is done in order that you may know, long before the time and while still on earth, that you are enrolled in heaven, and that your godfather who is in it is possessed of a great diligence to teach you, who are a stranger and newcomer to that great city, all the things that pertain to it.[8]

8. Theodore, quoted in Timothy A. Curtin, *The Baptismal Liturgy of Theodore of Mopsuestia*, Studies in Sacred Theology 222 (Washington, D.C.: The Catholic University Press, 1970), 92.

While Theodore sounds like he is rejecting the world, he is rather qualifying its authority, so that Christians learn to live as citizens of heaven in the midst of the earthly city. Using sponsors in the initiation process has a new importance in many churches today as they seek to reinvigorate mission in a post-Christian society.[9]

Spiritual direction has had a long history within monastic communities, but the practice waned in the West as therapy overtook traditional priestly guidance.[10] However, over the last thirty years, spiritual direction has come back as a major emphasis within mainstream Christianity.[11] Pastor and spiritual writer Eugene Peterson has contributed to this revival with his many books on pastoral leadership and the spiritual life.[12] His comments include both an encouragement and a warning:

> I'm a little bit uneasy about the professionalization of spiritual direction. Granted, the training and counsel can help us do this work better. But basically it's not a specialized thing. It's very much a part of the Christian life and should be very much a part of the pastor's life. In my view, spiritual direction is a conversation in which the pastor is taking the person seriously as a soul, as a creation of God for whom prayer is the most natural language.[13]

Guiding persons as souls, as creations of God, into the deeper journey of prayer and faithfulness in their day-to-day life: this is the model of

9. An excellent example of this is Lester Ruth, *Accompanying the Journey: A Handbook for Sponsors* (The Christian Initiation Series) (Nashville: Discipleship Resources, 1997).

10. A classic description of this trajectory is E. Brooks Holifield's *A History of Pastoral Care in America: From Salvation to Self-Realization* (Nashville: Abindgon, 1983). See also chapter three above.

11. See for an example of this trend the Shalem Institute for Spiritual Formation (http://www.shalem.org).

12. See, among others, Eugene Peterson, *The Contemplative Pastor: Returning to the Art of Spiritual Direction* (Grand Rapids: Eerdmans, 1993).

13. "The Best Life There Is: Eugene Peterson on Pastoral Ministry," interview by David Wood, *Christian Century*, March 13-20, 2002, 18-25.

spiritual direction called for in Peterson's writings and yearned for by countless persons of faith today.

I see two key components of the spiritual guide as a model for pastoral leaders that can be drawn out of the examples offered in part two of the book. First, *the pastoral leader as spiritual guide offers direction and guidance in enacting a practice.* Here pastoral leaders can guide communities into practices that embody the wisdom of how Christians live in the world now and how they have lived over the centuries. This pastoral leadership came to the fore in Gardiner, Maine, as Rob Webb and David Wood realized that eating together as Christians meant eating together with the poor and the lonely rather than simply with those we like. Learning how to engage in the practice, both in disposition and in the nuts and bolts of getting it done, came directly from the spiritual guidance Rob and David provided. It was absolutely essential that the meal be shared, rather than served by some to others, and essential as well that it be in their home, so to speak, as a congregation rather than some other place they didn't care about. Opening their church home, preparing a good meal, and sharing it with strangers marked the shape of this Christian practice.

Likewise, the other pastoral leaders gave direction and guidance to congregational practices that deepened their ability to connect faith to aspects of their lives day to day. Lillian both legitimated and modeled the practice of testimony by boldly offering her own moving testimony of a dramatic experience of one particular workplace. Mary provided a clear process within which to develop the ability for communal discernment, alternately pressing the group forward and stepping back to see where they would go next. Susan simply invited things usually not connected to come together with her blessing, turning sanctuary into jazz club and jazz into God's own song. In each case, these pastoral leaders found a practice that, even if practiced by the congregation gathered together, developed habits of heart and mind that take God's vision for life with them as they scatter into the world. Such practices, done together and over time, with wise guidance and focused rehearsal, equip the people of God with means to live faith day to day.

The second key component, however, is essential and integral to the first: *pastoral leaders as spiritual guides frame the meaning of the practice as the community enacts it.* In doing so, they draw resources from the biblical and theological languages of the Christian tradition to make sense of what the community is doing. This not only keeps the practice from being easily co-opted by the social and cultural obstacles the practice seeks to overcome; it also allows the community to see how such practices have parallels in other spheres of their lives. The meaning, then, is not the meaning of this practice alone, but the pattern it sets in an interconnected way throughout one's life. Again, in Gardiner, Maine, David Wood framed the meaning of table fellowship in terms of the eschatological kingdom of heaven, rooted in parables of Jesus in Scripture as well as prophetic and apocalyptic visions of God's Kingdom as it will be in its fullness. Such framing expands the imagination and gives a potentially broad impact for the simple practice of eating together.

Just as David seeks to unpack the theological meaning of the communal practice of eating together at First Baptist, the other pastoral leaders in the book in their own ways model theological reflection on the practices they encourage and lead. Lillian framed the problem of a Sunday-Monday gap and then offered a way of bringing God's claim on our lives to reflection about the circumstances of a particular workplace. Mary's insistence that Scripture is the basis for all we do, while not directly offering public policy recommendations, did clearly aim at discerning what the range of possible Christian responses might be. Susan brought to the jazz concerts her conviction about the church's identity as a community of hospitality and reconciliation given by God not simply for the congregation's own benefit, but for the sake of the city. In each case, these pastoral leaders reflected theologically on ordinary things the congregations do — work, read the newspaper, play and listen to music — pointing to the threads of our Christian faith already woven into daily actions and calling the congregation to practices through which God transforms their way of life.

Pastoral Leaders as Spiritual Guides
for Faith as a Way of Life

Dramatic stories of the growth of Pentecostalism globally and suburban megachurches in the United States, alongside reports of declining church membership within traditional mainline congregations, leave us with a lopsided view of the landscape in American Christianity.[14] As a step towards remedying this, Diana Butler Bass has described a new vitality emerging in traditional mainline congregations in the United States. Through an in-depth study of fifty congregations nationwide, she found that when these old "establishment churches" embrace renewed attention to their spiritual roots, they can emerge as vibrant congregations in and for the sake of their communities.[15] While her focus is not explicitly on pastoral leadership within these congregations, the patterns she identified resonate with the proposal I am developing in this book.

Butler Bass notes that cultural dislocations led to the demise of the small village of her youth. For generations her family lived, went to school, worked, and worshipped within a few blocks in a Baltimore neighborhood, but the United Methodist church of her youth has now declined along with the neighborhood. She tells this personal story as a parable of what happened to many churches in the United States over the past fifty years, a time of great upheaval and change in our society. In her provocative report on the new vitality of mainline churches, she shows how these historically liberal churches have returned to the traditional spiritual wellsprings that have given them

14. Allan Anderson, *An Introduction to Pentecostalism: Global Charismatic Christianity* (New York: Cambridge University Press, 2004); Stephen Ellingson, *The Megachurch and the Mainline: Remaking Religious Tradition in the Twenty-First Century* (Chicago: University of Chicago Press, 2007); David Roozen and James Nieman, eds., *Church, Identity and Change: Theology and Denominational Structures in Changing Times* (Grand Rapids: Eerdmans, 2005).

15. See Diana Butler Bass, *Christianity for the Rest of Us: How the Neighborhood Church Is Transforming the Faith* (New York: HarperSanFrancisco, 2006); as well as *The Practicing Congregation: Imagining a New Old Church* (Washington, D.C.: The Alban Institute, 2004).

life, offering space for seeking wisdom in community and fostering a way of life marked by practices of faith that draw people more deeply into being Christian.

How do pastoral leaders function within this emerging Christian church Butler Bass calls "the new village church"? They are very much the "spiritual guides" at the heart of these communities, recalling the tradition, gracefully welcoming seekers who desire God's wisdom for their lives, and fostering communal practices that are given by, and enacted as a response to, the God we know in Jesus Christ. Pastoral leaders are needed to foster a new sense of the vibrancy of the life of faith and of the local congregation as place of grace. Such faith offered, and such a congregational space prepared, allow those who feel fragmented and disconnected to become whole and engaged in community. They can grapple with the lively tension between their deepest beliefs and values and the life they live. Finding space and encouragement to ask the big, hard questions about work and its meaning, about how to raise children, about what abundance and success mean in life, about how individuals fit into community, makes the difference between feeling lost and feeling at home.[16]

Stories Tell It Best

Sometimes stories tell it best, and I've told a few stories of pastoral leadership along the way in this book. I'll conclude with two more. The subjects are intentionally quite different — one a Roman Catholic laywoman serving in campus ministry, and the other an ordained Congregational minister serving in a traditional local church. Both, however, are vibrant models of the sort of pastoral leadership this book seeks to foster. In offering a bit of their stories, I hope you will also begin to think of your story and how God is working in and through you for the sake of Christian faith lived in and for the life of the world.

---

16. See Butler Bass, *Christianity for the Rest of Us*, especially chapter four, "Finding Home," 55-70.

To Remain Alive in Our Faith

Catherine Brunell serves as a lay Roman Catholic campus minister at Boston College. Boston College, a major Jesuit university with nearly 15,000 students, sits in Chestnut Hill, a leafy, rolling suburb of Boston. Catherine is a "cradle Catholic." With twelve years of Catholic parochial school as well as a B.A. and M.A. from Boston College, she is well equipped to understand the challenges of working with young adults struggling to find a way to live their faith during their college years.

> The rich young man in Matthew's gospel has a conversation with Jesus that in my mind is asking — essentially what *does* a *lived* faith look like? The rich young man's question to Jesus was, "What must I do in order to gain eternal life?" He is inquiring about a rubric to apply to his life that would make it a life lived for God and therefore earn his place in the eternal Kingdom. He assures Jesus that he has been following all of the "rules" of his Jewish tradition but feels as if something is still missing. Jesus responds by beginning, "If you want to be perfect. . . ." Jesus is essentially reframing his question through perfection, but biblical scholars tell us that the "perfect" used is translated from the Greek *teleios* as whole or undivided.
>
> I have been Catholic all of my life, so I know that I should not eat an hour before mass. I know that birth control is considered a sin. I know that we do not sing "Alleluia" during the Lenten season and that women's ordination is prevented because a priest should be able to embody Christ and therefore needs to be male. The details of my faith, some that I trust and others that I do not, leave me in a similar place as the rich young man. With a burning desire to live a life that God has created me to live, I ask Jesus the same thing — "There is something more to a lived faith than following the rules of my tradition, isn't there?"

The fact is, however, that the combination of the marginalization of women in ministry combined with an overwhelming sense of how the church as an institution has failed people (the sexual abuse scandal and its cover-up by church leaders being only the most public recent example) creates huge obstacles for Catherine in answering the question about how to *have* faith, let alone how to live it and guide others in their faith journeys. With a busy new job in campus ministry, a new child at home, and the stress of such transitions eating her up, she took an important step. She decided that if she couldn't hear the merciful and loving call of God, and see where God's call was leading, she should find others who could help her.

The next step was building community. She had heard fellow Catholic women in her campus ministry office, and friends working elsewhere, express similar feelings of frustration and exhaustion. Catherine has a deep sense of hospitality and openness to others in her life. Taking a clue from this holy gift of hospitality, and building on the common insights she gained from conversations with colleagues, she decided that she should seek to build a small group of Catholic women working in campus ministry for encouragement in faith, for both personal and professional life.

The group began with a simple plan to gather monthly for prayer, discussion, and reflection on issues arising in their ministries and faith lives. Their hope was that if they could be spiritual guides for each other in the practice of theological reflection and discernment, they would be further grounded in their own faith as well as strengthened for guiding the students with whom they work. In each gathering, their process led them into specific questions about their everyday lives — at work, with family, in society. They wanted to understand what in their patterns of living was life-giving, faithful, and attuned to the Kingdom, as well as what drew them away from that very source of life they sought.

While they in theory were a group of twelve, too often work or family reduced the number, and they struggled to set aside the time to go deeper together. Ten months later, with a taste of how sustaining such connection could be, the group decided to take the plunge: they committed to a three-day retreat led by an experienced facilitator. Such an experience, Catherine thought, could give them all the space and focus

Invitation to a Faith as a Way of Life Small Group for Catholic Women Serving in Campus Ministry

Our collective experience suggests these areas of difficulty in our profession: translating the gospel message in relevant, practical, and lived ways to this generation of college-age students, staying afloat amidst taxing schedules and efforts to balance our work/family/personal commitments, negotiating the difficulty of multitasking programmatic logistics, email, and shared ministerial responsibilities while remaining present to the students and needs at hand, and the continual shifting between pastoral counseling and administrative tasks. These challenges invite the building of a deliberate and ongoing support network in order to remain alive in our faith and ministry.

to examine themselves and listen to one another with a real openness to God's voice and presence in their midst.

Held at the picturesque Conner's Family Retreat Center, a former Dominican priory along the Charles River, the retreat was a major breakthrough for the group. Reflecting on the experience of silence and speaking, prayer and laughter, personal sharing and spiritual direction, Catherine felt they practiced together the kind of ministry they all endeavored to share in their work and to live in their lives. Open to God's leading, they had found an authentic space to hear again God's love for them, to be transformed in their understanding of a call to serve the church, and even develop a renewed sense of what the church can be. One participant, Donna, said this: "I experienced a caring group of women in the Church who are an example of a small Church community. It seems to me that the retreat offered a sacred space to look at God who is the source of our energy and imagination. Spiritual nourishment for ourselves opens up the possibility of ministering in freedom." They found the space for small conversations, time for stories and laughter, time for silence in which to hear God, and through it all a kind of resonant authenticity they so often missed in their experiences of church.

Catherine is, in one sense, a pastoral leader who is leading to save her life. She knows that even if she is among tens of thousands of American lay professionals doing ministry in the Roman Catholic Church, she cannot simply wait for studies, programs of mentoring and support, and legitimation of authentic ministry status to emerge from the United States Council of Catholic Bishops.[17] In order to be effective in mentoring young people in their faith lives, she knows she needs to work together with peers. She notes that, while meeting with these women "was a smart thing to do professionally," she soon found it to be "much more than that." Giving testimony to how God has transformed her thinking through the mentoring of these other women, she now says, "I do not want to do ministry professionally. I want to live my ministry because it is my faith."

Drinking from a Fountain

Harold "Skip" Masback, a Congregational minister in the wealthy southwestern Connecticut hamlet of New Canaan, has ministered long enough in his community to know his congregants' captivity to high-powered, high-paying, high-pressure lifestyles. His description of the community is trenchant:

> We are the Congregational Church in the middle of the old New Canaan green. Folks are drawn to our church for all kinds of reasons. Some come simply because it looks like the place they want to be — where they want their daughter married. It is an extraordinarily prosperous, well credentialed and sometimes credential-driven community. Our church has a membership of 1830 people, with about 500 pre-confirmation children, and about 350 adoles-

17. Zeni Fox, *New Ecclesial Ministry: Lay Professionals Serving the Church,* revised and expanded ed. (Lanham, Md.: Sheed and Ward, 2002). The Catholic Church has officially — after much debate — agreed to use the term "minister" for certain categories of lay people. Still, Catherine notes, "without a collar, my thoughts are often sub-par in the circles that even sometimes invite my voice."

cents in our youth group. We average 400 people on Sunday. We have a church within a church. We have a group of 700 in the church who probably try earnestly to attend when they are in town. Within this there is a church within a church within a church of about 150 folks who consistently throw themselves into the full range of church community offerings. Most of our real congregational support comes from these committed folks.

Our congregation is quite diverse in terms of theological understanding. We can preach three sermons on grace and still have some people who want to start a committee to get grace. Some in our congregation have very thin catechism background and little biblical background. So we try to offer programs that are recognized as urgent needs in their life. We have to make the sale with respect to the urgent problem and make it clear that faith and the Christian tradition are relevant. For some, the decision to participate in adult education events is framed as a "consumer" issue, and they wonder whether a local minister has the requisite credentials to justify their commitment. Sometimes we play into consumer aspirations by bringing in Ivy League divinity school professors as marquee "draws." We then have trouble arranging times that people can actually attend: 6:30 A.M. is too late for the commuters and 7:30 P.M. is too early — the majority of the breadwinners work in Manhattan, taking the commuter train in daily.

As Skip and his associate pastor, Alan Hilton, began to mull over how to engage their congregation in deepening their life of faith, they thought big. Through a multi-year process to incorporate their church into the vision of faith as a way of life, they reasoned that they could offer the community — and its members individually — the opportunity to discern the larger purpose of their lives and gradually make moves to bring their lives into greater alignment with this purpose.

Their problem, as Skip mentions above, was how to sell the idea to people who have already achieved so much of what can be achieved, who already own so much of what can be owned. Skip knew that the community members had deep issues with fulfillment and joy, so he

An Invitation to a Way of Life

Jesus once summed up his mission on earth in a single sentence: "I came that they may have life and have it abundantly" (John 10:10). Do these words surprise you? Jesus doesn't want our faith to be the dutiful endurance of an obligatory hour of church each week or grudging consent to a list of irrelevant dogmas. He wants faith to be the source of our deepest joy and our greatest passion — our very life blood.

"Faith as a Way of Life" is for people who want the real deal, not the religious trappings. It is for people who agree that if Jesus offers us the water of life, we'd rather drink it from a fountain than through a dropper. "Faith as a Way of Life" will help us to open more and more of ourselves — our relationships, our activities, even our attitudes — to God. What could be better than experiencing the rich love of God all the way to the very boundaries of our being?

— New Canaan Congregational Church

started there. The people want to know what's missing in their lives, what church can add to their already crowded schedules. The church's reply was to teach the gospel as a story about Jesus' promise of abundant life and joy. The admitted risk was that they would simply feed the kind of narcissism in which people already think all God wants is their own good — a kind of divinely mandated self-maximization. So instead they raised the question of how sin — individually and corporately — blocks God's desire for humans and all creation to live the abundant life Jesus offered. They emphasized the need to serve others and find meaning in service — both locally and through congregational mission trips. Overall, they have worked over a number of years emphasizing relationships among friends and family; work, Sabbath, use of leisure time, service as vocation, money and leadership; and community life as it bears the fruits of the spirit, repentance and grace.

Skip has a special heart for young people and has, despite his wide range of responsibilities as senior minister, kept a close connection to the young people of the congregation. I joined him one night during Quest, a sub-group of the much larger group for high-school-age youth. Quest is for those who want to explore deeper spiritual practice, prayer, and friendship. This week I showed up at 5:30, since Skip was meeting four or five youth every week for dinner beforehand. His aim? Listen, ask questions, and learn about their lives, their loves, their worries and hopes. We sat together at the restaurant and bantered about college admission jitters, upcoming tests at school, and excitement for the mission trip to Belize coming in May. Later, as we gathered in the church, the group welcomed a few alumni home for spring break and settled down to comfortable positions on the floor for prayer, silence, and reflection on messages of faith and life in songs I'd brought to play for them. We reflected together about how the stories in these songs — about faith in the face of doubt and hope in the face of suffering — touched their stories. We concluded by praying for one another, for people near and far who were suffering, and for the gift of life and community, of God's love and presence. Skip closed, hugs were shared, and most of us headed down the street to Baskin-Robbins to celebrate a couple birthdays with ice cream — Skip's treat.

Skip and his associate pastors have offered their parishioners a robust and expansive vision: that the life they live is not really abundant life until they give it away, to each other and to those they do not know. The particular complexity of his community shapes his strategic thinking about the best ways to make the pitch and gives him ample reason to worry about potential pitfalls. Yet he has listened well to his people and to God, coming to a compelling message of the free offer of life abundant, life that does not have to be clamored for and grasped, but which flows to and beyond us free as a flowing fountain of refreshing water. Through his preaching on Sundays, framing the adult and youth education programs, planning mission trips, and encouraging individuals, Skip embodies the pastoral leader as spiritual guide. He has invited people to practice their faith daily, as a way of life. He has invited them to do this through worship, study, keeping Sabbath, eating together, and more, and has framed it all in terms the congregation will easily understand. He said to them: do you think you know what it means to experience joy, to find rest, to be filled? Think again, and come share the joy, rest, and fullness of God. Through his attentive and repetitive coaxing and inviting style, the community has caught hold of this vision.

Finally . . .

Finally, pastoral leadership depends on our standing before God as beggars. Leadership for faith as a way of life is not a skill set achieved through attending seminars and buying attractive program resources to implement in your place of ministry. No, the invitation here is more elemental; it is more biblical, at once harder and easier than some achievement model of ministry excellence. Pastoral leaders like Skip and Catherine want and need to be effective spiritual guides for fellow disciples on the way.

This book offers no easy steps that mask the difficult work of ministry. Instead it attempts to clear away the obstacles that prevent us from seeing the height and depth and breadth of God's gift of grace and mercy in Christ Jesus that by the power of the Spirit turns us from death to life. We are exactly beggars as we stand before this God, whose power to save alone sets us upon the way to life abundant. In God's action turning us from death to life, we find our task: exercising the faith given to us as disciples and as leaders, shaping communities of discipleship, living our faith as a way of life in and for the sake of the world. May God prosper the work of your hands as you receive the gift of faith and exercise it in your pastoral leadership.

Subject-Name Index

Scripture Index